Empowerment for Girls

Riveting Reads for Primary Schools

BARBARA BAND

FOREWORD: SALLY NICHOLLS

SERIES EDITOR: CATHAL COYLE

School Library Association

Acknowledgements

The author would like to thank all the school librarians, throughout the UK and worldwide, who share their love, knowledge and passion for books so readily. They have been, and continue to be, an inspiration and I hope this publication helps them to inspire others. I dedicate it to my grandchildren; may they grow up to be empowered and empathetic.

Published by

School Library Association
1 Pine Court, Kembrey Park
Swindon SN2 8AD

Tel: 01793 530166
E-mail: info@sla.org.uk
Web: www.sla.org.uk

Registered Charity No: 313660
Charity Registered in Scotland No: SC039453

© School Library Association 2019. All rights reserved.
ISBN: 978-1-911222-22-4

Printed by Holywell Press, Oxford

Cover image by Pete Linforth from Pixabay

Contents

Foreword by Sally Nicholls 4

Introduction 5

Resources 8

Riveting Reads

    Picture Books 9

    Fiction Books 18

    Information Books 28

    Graphic Novels and Manga 42

Index of Authors 49

Index of Illustrators 51

Index of Titles 52

Series editor's note: The ISBN numbers given in this publication are indicative of currently available titles; other editions and formats may be available.

Foreword
by Sally Nicholls

We live in a patriarchal society and sadly, the books we give to our children reflect that. A study analysing the 100 bestselling picture books in Britain in 2017 found that male characters were twice as likely to take leading roles than women. On average, three male characters were present for every two females.

And where males were present, they were more likely to be fierce, strong or villainous, taking parts such as monsters, tigers and lions, while girls were more likely to be mothers, or small, vulnerable animals such as insects or birds ('prey' as one commentator noticed). There was only one female villain in the entire sample, and that was a duck which stole Peppa Pig's Wellingtons.

Even when books get it right, parents manage to screw it up – another study showed that when parents read to a child, they will refer to any characters or animal without an explicit gender as 'he'. This is something I definitely notice myself doing when reading to my children (see also teddy bears, babies, cats and bumble bees.) Despite my feminist credentials, my three-year-old refers to everyone as 'he'. Including his grandmother.

It's not just in fiction that women are marginalised. The 2017 *Drawing the Future* report analysed sixty-six drawings of fire-fighters, surgeons, and pilots in children's books, and found that sixty-one were of men and five of women. Another study found that in children's science books, scientists were three times more likely to be depicted as male than female.

Can't we as parents, writers and educators do better than this? We certainly can. The books in this collection have been hand-picked to challenge the gender assumptions girls – and boys – grow up with. They celebrate female heroines, female figures from history and public life, and female role models. They offer girls a different story to centre themselves in, and it's about time too.

These stories – and others like them – are necessary, not just for girls, but for boys too. Boys need to stop thinking of themselves as monsters and girls as prey. They need to learn to value things which are traditionally female as much as things which are traditionally male. We need to acknowledge that patriarchy is created by boys and girls, and those of us who raise and educate them, and that dismantling it is work that we all share.

These books aren't just for young girls. They're for everyone.

Sally Nicholls
Children's Book Author

Introduction

One of the ways we make sense about 'who we are' and our place in the world is via our gender. What society considers 'normal' for boys and girls impacts on how we treat them and children pick up on this in the way they dress, act and behave. Children imitate what they see, they try and replicate what is expected of them and if we treat girls and boys differently, albeit subconsciously, they will see themselves as different. There are both visible and invisible gender-biased influences on children from their early years that impact on their life choices and that have long-term effects.

Gender stereotyping begins before birth with prospective parents being channelled into the blue or pink route, often because there isn't any other choice. Research shows that, at only 3 to 4 months, babies can distinguish between male and female faces. A few months later and they link voices to those faces, and by the time they are only ten months old, they link stereo-typical objects to gender. Thus early gender stereotypes have a huge role to play.

Children learn about the world through reading and the media – particularly the images they see and the messages they hear. If these are constantly gender-biased they send a strong signal reinforcing gender inequality, and a message that boys and girls not only are different, but should also be treated differently. This continual reinforcement via childhood, school and society results in an assumption that this is how it should be and that male dominance is the norm, and will affect how children respond to each other.

The idea that specific toys, colours and activities are for specific genders is a marketing concept aimed at generating additional sales. However, these gender ideas have now become established and there is a societal cost to breaking the 'norm' for both the parent and the child; there is a strong argument that we need to counteract this.

Approximately 50% of the world's population is female[1] and this section of society will help to make up our future workforce of leaders, scientists, mathematicians and engineers. If we rely on the male 50% to fulfil these roles we are losing a lot of potential, and a huge source of creativity and inspiration that is important for the future of our society.

Girls are constantly being given the message that:

- STEM subjects are 'for boys' so they are not considering them for further or higher education. One in twenty girls considers a STEM career compared to one in five boys.
- Girls do not lead and play a supporting role in any initiative or project.
- They are vulnerable and should be quiet and 'look pretty' as it is the boys' job to be the hero and rescue you or save the day.
- Men are worth more.
- Physical appearance is more important than academic achievements.

In 2017, an *Observer* study carried out by Nielsen Market Research Company, undertook an in-depth analysis of the 100 most popular children's picture books.[2] the results were interesting:

- Male characters were twice as likely to take leading roles and be given far more speaking parts
- 20% of the books had no female characters.
- When animals were used as characters, 73% were more likely to be male than female.

---

[1] https://data.worldbank.org/indicator/SP.POP.TOTL.FE.ZS

[2] https://www.theguardian.com/books/2018/jan/21/childrens-books-sexism-monster-in-your-kids-book-is-male

- Male animals were portrayed as powerful and wild such as dragons and tigers whilst female animals were quiet and weak such as rabbits and cats.

- Male villains were eight times more likely to appear than female villains.

- The characters portrayed very stereotypical roles, for example, the females were in the kitchen or looking after the children whilst the men fought battles or went to work.

One example of a dominant male is okay but it is a problem if the majority of male characters in books are represented in that way; likewise if every female character is a sidekick or placed in a domestic environment, this is not sending an affirmative or constructive message.

There have been a lot of books published to coincide with the 100th anniversary of 'Votes for Women' and the publishing world is slowly changing. For example, Ladybird no longer brands books as 'for girls' or 'for boys' but there is still a way to go. Older books with stereotypical characters remain family favourites so are still bought and read. Schools and libraries do not have the budget to replace older books with new ones depicting strong resilient female characters.

All children need to see themselves in books — in both fiction and non-fiction — and they should be able to explore various role models. They can only aspire to what they know exists, as the adage goes 'you can't be what you can't see,' so if a child never sees themselves represented in anything other than a 'traditional role' they will assume that anything outside the box is not for them.

The world shrinks for girls which means we need to ensure that they are aware of all their options. There is nothing wrong with pink or unicorns. There is nothing wrong with blue or dinosaurs. But children should have the choice of blue unicorns or pink dinosaurs.

Gender inequality has long-term consequences for girls:

- Girls' better test scores do not translate into equality at home, in the workplace or in society

- There is a lack of confidence amongst girls — women tend to only apply for jobs if they have 100% of the criteria

- The gender pay gap exists; 78% of companies pay men more[3]

- Women are underrepresented within STEM, business and politics

- Girls tend to focus on their appearance and are under pressure to conform.

What can you do?

While it is not possible to remove every gender stereotypical influence, it is important to challenge them, and we can help by creating a more balanced approach within our libraries and with the books we offer children:

- Ensure there is a fair representation of males and females — not only amongst book stock but also when creating displays. Do you ensure your display has a range of male and female authors? Do your books have a range of male and female protagonists in a variety of roles?

- When giving book talks, make certain you have a balanced mix of male and female authors and protagonists. And include female villains! This goes the same for reading lists.

- When supporting national events, such as Black History Month or Science Week, have you promoted equal numbers of males and females? Displays about scientists should not be all about white men. There are plenty of excellent female role models that can be included. It may

---

[3] https://www.bbc.co.uk/news/business-43668187

be that material isn't readily available, in which case it is a simple matter to create your own posters and fact sheets. Have a look at some of the book suggestions to give you some ideas.

■ Think about the language and words you use both when talking to children and in displays as words affect us all. We would never think of calling somebody a 'working dad' and yet the phrase 'working mum' is used all the time.

■ Swap pronouns when reading out loud. If no gender is mentioned, check your default option isn't 'he'.

■ Think about how you present gender in the library. Do you have lists of 'top ten books borrowed by girls/boys'? Consider removing the gender and produce lists relating to tutor or year groups.

■ Allocate tasks fairly between boys and girls. Make sure girls are not always the ones tidying up and sorting or that boys are always the ones carrying or moving.

■ Create an environment where girls feel they are safe to 'fail' and where they will not fear 'getting it wrong'. If they have an environment where they do not feel secure, it will impact on their self-confidence.

■ Validate their choices. It is not wrong to be interested in clothes or make-up or to like pink. It is the range of choice available that is important.

How to use this guide

The book suggestions are divided into the following categories:

■ Picture books

■ Fiction books

■ Non-fiction books

■ Graphic novels and Manga.

Each book has been given a suggested age range. However, as children vary in their emotional maturity as well as their reading levels and capacity for inference, these are only recommendations. The age recommendation often depends on the content rather than the reading level and a book suitable for a child of '10–12 years' may not be appropriate for a more able eight-year-old reader.

All the picture books are listed for 'Under 8 years (KS1)' but many of them would make an excellent starting point for discussion with older children. Some of the books have a listing with both '8–12' and '12–14'; these are obviously aimed at the older end of KS2 and I would advise you to investigate the book and subject matter before recommending it to a child.

As with any book recommendation, ideally you need to know the reader, their background and the issues they are dealing with – and then use your professional judgement as to whether it is suitable. If in doubt, read the book yourself first.

All the titles listed were in print at the time of compiling this guide. There are some excellent books published that had to be omitted due to lack of space; and no doubt, more have been published since. Some of those listed may also now be available in paperback.

Gender stereotyping applies as equally to boys as to girls, and boys are under as much pressure to conform to the 'norm' of being strong, 'manning up' and not showing emotions. In the same way that both sexes need to see equal and empowering female role models in books – both sexes also need to see kind and nurturing male role models.

Resources

- British Council
  https://www.britishcouncil.org/society/womens-and-girls-empowerment

- Girl Guiding
  https://www.girlguiding.org.uk/social-action-advocacy-and-campaigns/social-action-and-campaigns/

- Girls Out Loud
  http://girlsoutloud.org.uk/

- Let Toys Be Toys
  http://lettoysbetoys.org.uk

- A Mighty Girl
  https://amightygirl.com

- NEU: Challenging Gender Stereotypes
  https://www.teachers.org.uk/equality/equality-matters/breaking-mould

- United Nations Gender Equality goals
  https://www.un.org/sustainabledevelopment/gender-equality/

- Women In the World
  https://womenintheworld.com

- World Vision
  https://www.worldvision.org/gender-equality-news-stories/seven-ways-empower-women-girls

Picture Books

ACE, LAUREN

Illustrated by Jenny Løvlie

The Girls

Caterpillar Books, 2018   ISBN: 9781848577190

Four little girls become friends and form a bond that stays with them as they grow up. This book follows each of them as the years pass and they share secrets and worries, achieve their dreams and ambitions. With a range of diverse and adventurous characters that grow into strong women, this is an excellent book to encourage resilience and an independent spirit. **Under 8**

BEATY, ANDREA

Illustrated by David Roberts

Ada Twist, Scientist

Abrams Books, 2016   ISBN: 9781419721373

Ada has a boundless curiosity for science, continually conducts experiments, is constantly asking how things work and her favourite question is 'why'. So when her house fills with an awful smell she knows it's down to her to find the source. The rhyming text and large colour illustrations make this a perfect book to read aloud. **Under 8**

See also:

Rosie Revere, Engineer

Abrams Books, 2013   ISBN: 9781419708459

BECKER, AARON

Journey

Walker Books, 2014   ISBN: 9781406355345

A little girl draws a magic door on her bedroom wall and escapes through it into a world full of wonder. Exquisitely illustrated, this wordless picture book tells a tale of friendship, kindness, adventure and determination. **Under 8**

See also:

Quest

Walker Books, 2015   ISBN: 9781406360813

Return

Walker Books, 2017   ISBN: 9781406373295

BENJAMIN, FLOELLA

Illustrated by Margaret Chamberlain

My Two Grannies

Frances Lincoln, 2009   ISBN: 9781847800343

Alvira has two grannies; one from the Caribbean, the other from the UK. When both move in to look after her whilst her parents are on holiday, there is a clash of cultures. However, Alvira thinks of a solution to the situation which ensures the grannies become best friends. **Under 8**

BRYAN, KERRINE and BRYAN, JASON

Illustrated by Marissa Penguinho

My Mummy Is an Engineer

Butterfly Books, 2015   ISBN: 9780993276903

This is the first title in a series of career-themed picture books that challenge stereotypes. As well as introducing children to various fields of engineering via rhyming words, the engineer is a mummy who ensures her children have a bedtime story at the end of the day. **Under 8**

See also:

My Mummy Is a Plumber

Butterfly Books, 2015   ISBN: 9780993276927

My Mummy Is a Scientist

Butterfly Books, 2016   ISBN: 9780993276941

COELHO, JOSEPH

Illustrated by Fiona Lumbers

Luna Loves Library Day

Andersen Press, 2017   ISBN: 9781783445486

Luna's favourite day of the week is when she sees her dad and they visit the library together to sit on the big library chair and share books. A charming and poignant story that illustrates the importance of family, showing a non-stereotypical father, and the enrichment of books and reading. **Under 8**

COLE, BABETTE

Princess Smartypants

Puffin, 1996   ISBN: 9780140555264

Princess Smartypants is rich, pretty and, most definitely, does not want to get married. However, all the princes have other ideas and try, one by one, to convince her otherwise. An amusing tale that teaches girls that you can be a princess but also still be independent. **Under 8**

CORDELL, MATTHEW

Wolf in the Snow

Macmillan, 2017   ISBN: 9781250076366

A little girl, walking home from school in a snowy blizzard, finds a lost wolf cub. Using the cries of the pack as a guide, she carries it across fields and streams to return it to its family but then collapses. The wolves stay by her side, howling and guarding her, until her parents arrive to save her. A wordless picture book that portrays a tale of kindness and bravery. **Under 8**

COWELL, CRESSIDA

That Rabbit Belongs to Emily Brown

Hodder Children's Books, 2015ISBN: 9781444923414

Emily Brown is strong-minded, adventurous and doesn't take no for an answer. When the Queen sends the footmen, army, navy and airforce to take Emily's rabbit, Stanley, she's not going to let her get away with it. Bold, captivating illustrations and fun repetitive text make this an enjoyable book to read aloud. **Under 8**

DOCHERTY, HELEN and DOCHERTY, THOMAS
The Snatchabook

Alison Green Books, 2013   ISBN: 9781407116549

Eliza Brown is perplexed when, one evening, her book disappears. After discovering this is happening across Burrow Down, she decides to investigate despite being unsure about what type of monster is stealing everyone's books. When she discovers it's a Snatchabook she swallows her fears, hatches a plan to put things right and get everyone's books back again. **Under 8**

DONALDSON, JULIA

Illustrated by Alex Scheffler

Zog

Alison Green Books, 2016   ISBN: 9781407170763

Zog is an accident-prone dragon. Fortunately, there's a little girl on hand to patch up his wounds; a princess who doesn't need rescuing by a knight and who would much rather be a doctor. A great story about breaking free of stereotypes and perfect for reading aloud. **Under 8**

FALCONER, IAN
Olivia and the Fairy Princesses

Simon & Schuster, 2013   ISBN: 9781471117756

Olivia is determined, strong-willed and not at all impressed that everyone in her class seems to want to be a princess. Pink and sparkly is just 'not' her! She wants to be different and stand out so sets off on a hilarious quest to find a princess she can identify with. A wonderful picture book that explores the many ways you can be a princess, and be yourself, without being the same as everyone else. **Under 8**

FOREMAN, MICHAEL
Newspaper Boy and Origami Girl

Andersen Press, 2013   ISBN: 9781849395199

When a group of bullies steals Joey's money, his bag of newspapers suddenly transforms into Origami Girl who whisks him off on an adventurous chase to get his money back. **Under 8**

See also:
The Little Bookshop and the Origami Army

Anderson Press, 2017   ISBN: 9781783442089

FUNKE, CORNELIA

Illustrated by Kasia Matyjaszek

Molly Rogers, Pirate Girl

Barrington Stoke, 2017   ISBN: 9781781126929

When Captain Firebeard and his crew capture Molly, they more than meet their match. She knows the real pirate to fear is none other than her mum, who won't be very happy when she discovers Molly has been kidnapped. A swashbuckling adventure about a small feisty girl. **Under 8**

GARZA, LUCINDA LEONOR

Illustrated by Alyssa Bermudez

Lucinda the Luchadora

Pow! 2017   ISBN: 9781576878279

Lucinda is not impressed when the boys at school tell her she can't be a superhero because she's a girl. But her abuela reveals that she comes from a long line of strong and courageous women, the Mexican lucha libre, who fight for what is right but never reveal their identity. When she notices a classmate being bullied, Lucinda has to decide whether she will reveal her identity and stand up for them or keep quiet. **Under 8**

GOODHART, PIPPA

Illustrated by Marjan Vafaian

The Parrot and the Merchant

Tiny Owl Publishing, 2017   ISBN: 9781910328255

Mah Jahan is a wealthy merchant who keeps colourful birds in cages. When she sets off for India, she promises that she'll visit the jungle on behalf of her favourite parrot and ask his friends if they have any messages for him. She is rather surprised at their response when she does this. A story about how to treat others. **Under 8**

HART, CARYL

Illustrated by Ali Pye

Girls Can Do Anything

Scholastic, 2018   ISBN: 9781407177380

A rhyming picture book that shows girls really can be and do anything – from climbing mountains to becoming Prime Minister, from being neat to being scruffy. There is no right or wrong way of being a girl. **Under 8**

HART, CARYL

Illustrated by Sarah Warburton

The Princess and the Christmas Rescue

Nosy Crow, 2017   ISBN: 9780857639783

Princess Eliza is brilliant at making toys and gadgets but is lonely stuck in her palace with no-one to play with. When Santa becomes ill, she steps in to help the stressed-out and panicking elves, and manages to find some friends along the way. An inspirational story about being strong and individual. **Under 8**

HOFFMAN, MARY

Illustrated by Caroline Binch

Amazing Grace

Frances Lincoln Children's Books, 2007   ISBN: 9781845077495

Grace thinks she can be anything or anyone but her classmates inform her she can't be Peter Pan because she's a girl and is black. However, her grandmother shows her a positive role model that convinces her to try out for the school play audition. She wins the part and is a success. **Under 8**

HOWARTH, NAOMI
The Night Dragon

Lincoln Children's Books, 2018 ISBN: 9781786031037

Maud, a beautifully-coloured dragon, is picked on by the other dragons because she is too scared to fly and fill the sky with sooty clouds that bring on the night. When they fall asleep after a party, her friend Mouse convinces her she can take on the task. A wonderful story about friendship and believing in yourself. **Under 8**

ISMAIL, YASMEEN
I'm a Girl!

Bloomsbury Children's Books, 2015 ISBN: 9781408857007

The girl in this book is always being mistaken for a boy because she likes to wear shorts, and is fast and strong. Then she meets a boy who likes wearing dresses and playing dolls, and they realise they have a lot in common. Illustrated with bright vibrant images, this book sends a positive message about being who you are. **Under 8**

ISMAIL, YASMEEN
Nothing!

Bloomsbury Children's Books, 2016 ISBN: 9781408873366

Mummy and Lila are off to visit Grandpa but Lila is busy in her own imaginary world and gets distracted by so many exciting things — racing in chariots, flying with birds, battling sea monsters — a celebration of imaginary play. **Under 8**

JONES, PIP
Illustrated by Sara Ogilvie

Izzy Gizmo

Simon & Schuster Children's Books, 2017 ISBN: 9780857075130

Izzy loves to invent things and always carries her toolbag around with her in case she discovers something that needs to be mended. However, her efforts never turn out the way she intended which makes her very cross. Then she finds a crow with a broken wing — can she put her frustrations aside to help him? A fun story told in rhyme. **Under 8**

KEMP, ANNA
Illustrated by Sara Ogilvie

The Worst Princess

Simon & Schuster, 2012 ISBN: 9781847388766

A feminist retelling of the Rapunzel story in which the princess realises the prince who comes to save her is a bit of a drip so she decides to go off and have adventures with the dragon. A great antidote to traditional princess stories with detailed pictures and amusing text. **Under 8**

KILBRIDE, SARAH

Illustrated by Ada Grey

Being a Princess Is Very Hard Work

Bloomsbury, 2018   ISBN: 9781408881934

If you're going to be a princess then you have to be clean, not pick your nose and have perfect table manners – it's quite hard work. However, one princess' parents decide that being yourself – noisy, messy, kind and generous – is much better. A book that sends a message about being yourself rather than what everyone else wants to be. **Under 8**

KNAPMAN, TIMOTHY

Illustrated by Joe Berger

Superhero Mum

Nosy Crow, 2018   ISBN: 9781788001441

All mums are brilliant and this mum is no exception. She goes through the day finding missing toys, running superfast to catch the bus and carrying bags of really heavy shopping. A book that illustrates the multitude of tasks mums do, often seemingly with ease. **Under 8**

KOKIAS, KERRI

Illustrated by Teagan White

Snow Sisters

Alfred A Knopf, 2018   ISBN: 9781101938836

It's a snowy day outside and two sisters react very differently; one dashes outside to play, the other stays indoors. When they swap places and follow in each other's footsteps, they each put their own spin on the activities. A story about being different, with the mirrored text and detailed illustrations inviting discussion. **Under 8**

LENTON, STEVEN

Princess Daisy and the Dragon and the Nincompoop Knights

Nosy Crow, 2015   ISBN: 9780857632883

Princess Daisy knows just how to stop the loud scary sound that is waking the kingdom up every night. But her father won't listen to her because she's a girl and, instead, calls for the knights. When they all prove to be easily scared nincompoops, along comes a mysterious knight who dares to enter the dragon's den. Great book for rewriting stereotypes about girls being helpless and clueless. **Under 8**

LEW-VRIETHOFF, JOANNE and MCANULTY, STACY

Beautiful

Running Press Kids, 2016   ISBN: 9780762457816

This book explores the ways in which everyone is unique and that by being yourself you can be strong, smart and beautiful. It celebrates potential and breaks down gender stereotypes featuring a range of girls with various skin colours, body types and abilities doing activities that are often consider 'male'. **Under 8**

LOEWEN, MARK

Illustrated by Ed Pokoj

What Does a Princess Really Look Like?

Boutique of Quality Books, 2018   ISBN: 9781945448171

Chloe wants to be a princess ballerina and draws her own version with the help of her two dads. Doing this she discovers that being a princess isn't just about having a sparkly dress but also involves the qualities needed to be unique, strong and self-confident. **Under 8**

NOLEN, JERDINE

Illustrated by Elise Primavera

Raising Dragons

Houghton Mifflin, 2002   ISBN: 9780152165369

When a little girl, living on a farm, finds an egg that hatches into a dragon she decides to keep it and raise it. They have many adventures together but, despite the dragon being useful and helping with the farm duties, her parents believe the best place for him is in dragon country. Sadly, she takes him away but, on her return, discovers there are more eggs waiting for a dragon raiser! **Under 8**

PETT, MARK and RUBINSTEIN, GARY

Illustrated by Mark Pett

The Girl Who Never Made Mistakes

Sourcebooks, 2012   ISBN: 9781402255441

Beatrice Bottomwell, age 9, has never made a mistake and holds the record of perfection in her home town. But then, one day, she makes a very public mistake – and learns that making mistakes is okay and that you don't have to be perfect to have fun. **Under 8**

REYNOLDS, PETER H.

The Dot (Creatology)

Walker Books, 2004   ISBN: 9781844281695

Vashti says she can't draw but her teacher thinks she can. When Vashti makes an angry dot on her paper, her teacher encourages her to sign it which leads to all sorts of creative imaginings. A book with the message that we can all be creative and that sometimes we just have to believe in ourselves and try. **Under 8**

RIDDELL, CHRIS

Once Upon a Wild Wood

Macmillan Children's Books, 2018   ISBN: 9781509817061

Little Green Cape is on her way to Rapunzel's party. On the journey she meets a myriad of familiar fairy-tale characters but is smart enough to outwit them all. Children will love spotting and identifying their favourite stories. **Under 8**

SPIRES, ASHLEY
The Most Magnificent Thing

Kids Can Press, 2017   ISBN: 9781554537044

A little girl decides to make a most magnificent 'thing'. However, it is not easy and after trying and failing, she gives up. Her best friend, a dog, convinces her to take a walk and she comes back with renewed enthusiasm. A funny book, which illustrates the rewards of creativity and perseverance as well as demonstrating that it is okay to make mistakes, with a wonderful use of exploratory language to describe actions. **Under 8**

UEGAKI, CHIERI

Illustrated by Qin Leng

Hana Hashimoto, Sixth Violin

Kids Can Press, 2015   ISBN: 9781894786331

Hana has only just started to learn how to play the violin and yet still wants to enter the school's talent competition. Her brothers insist she's not good enough. But Hana remembers how her grandfather in Japan used to practise the violin every day so she does the same and surprises everyone, including herself, when she comes to perform. A story about resilience, perseverance and having the confidence to not let anyone tell you that you can't do something. **Under 8**

VALENTINE, RACHEL

Illustrated by Katie Weyworth

Audrey the Amazing Inventor

Words & Pictures, 2018   ISBN: 9781910277584

Audrey wants to be an inventor but nothing she creates seems to work. She's ready to give up but after encouraging words decides to carry on with her dream. **Under 8**

VAN DUSEN, CHRIS
Hattie and Hudson

Candlewick Press, 2017   ISBN: 9780763665456

Every morning, Hattie sets off in her canoe to explore the lake. One day her singing attracts a huge mysterious beast and everyone is terrified. However, Hattie knows that Hudson, as she has called him, is friendly and gentle but how can she make the townspeople see this? A story about not judging anyone by their looks or size. **Under 8**

WILLIS, JEANNE

Illustrated by Briony May Smith

Stardust

Nosy Crow, 2017   ISBN: 9781788000680

One little girl dreams of being a star but is always overshadowed by her big sister. However, her Grandad explains that the whole world is made of stardust and that she's always a star to him. This message and the self-confidence it creates sticks as the final page sees the little girl, now a woman, heading for the stars as an astronaut. **Under 8**

WOODWARD, KAY

Illustrated by Jo De Ruiter

Sleeping Handsome and the Princess Engineer

Curious Fox, 2015   ISBN: 9781782023128

In this retelling of Sleeping Beauty, it's a prince who pricks his finger and falls asleep only to be rescued by a Princess Anya, an engineer complete with her own tunnelling machine. Certainly not a damsel in distress, she brushes aside his proposal and suggests they go to the cinema instead. An amusing story illustrated by detailed drawings in a pastel spectrum. **Under 8**

WOOLVIN, BETHAN

Little Red

Two Hoots, 2017   ISBN: 9781447291404

Little Red Riding Hood meets a wolf on her way to visit her sick grandmother. He's hungry so he gobbles up Grandma and lies in wait but this little girl isn't so easily fooled and has a plan to thwart the wolf - something he certainly didn't bargain for. A darker version of the traditional tale, with almost graphic illustrations and sparse text, which will thrill those already familiar with the story. **Under 8**

See also:

Rapunzel

Two Hoots, 2018   ISBN: 9781509842681

Fiction Books

ATINUKE

Illustrated by Lauren Tobia

You're Amazing, Anna Hibiscus!

Walker Books, 2016   ISBN: 9781406349139

Anna Hibiscus is a little girl who lives in Africa with her extended family including baby twin brothers, Double and Trouble. Through these books we learn about her life in the city, the village where her grandparents grew up, visiting the market and going to school. In this book, the eighth and final one in the series, Anna is worried about her brothers who can't keep out of trouble and her grandfather who is tired all the time. A lovely series with diverse characters. **Under 8**

BARNHILL, KELLY

The Girl Who Drank the Moon

Piccadilly Press, 2017   ISBN: 9781848126473

Every year the people of Protectorate leave a baby out as a sacrifice for the witch, hoping to keep her from terrorising the town. But the witch saves the babies, feeding them with starlight and placing them with loving families on the other side of the forest. One year she accidentally feeds a baby with moonlight, making her magical, so decides to raise Luna herself. As Luna's thirteenth birthday approaches, her magic emerges with dangerous consequences. A fantasy story with a diverse range of characters. **8–12**

BELL, ALEX

Illustrated by Tomislav Tomac

The Polar Bear Explorer's Club

Faber & Faber, 2018   ISBN: 9780571332540

As Stella and her fellow female explorers trek across the wild snowy wastes they have to face dangers and threats. A thrilling magical adventure about bravery and friendship involving frost fairies, snow queens, unicorns and pygmy dinosaurs. **8–12**

BLACKMAN, MALORIE

Illustrated by Jamie Smith

Betsey Biggalow and the Detective

Red Fox, 2014   ISBN: 9781782951841

This book is one of five short story collections featuring Betsey, who lives in Barbados with her family. During her adventures she shows you don't have to be big to make a difference. There are four stories in each book making them ideal for building reading confidence. **Under 8**

See also:

Betsey Biggalow Is Here!

Red Fox, 2014   ISBN: 9781782951858

Betsey Biggalow's Birthday Surprise

Red Fox, 2014   ISBN: 9781782951889

Magic Betsey

Red Fox, 2014   ISBN: 9781782951872

BLACKMAN, MALORIE
Thief!

Corgi Children's, 2004   ISBN: 9780552551656

When Lydia starts at a new school she is set up by a girl gang, accused of theft and bullied. Running away she gets lost on the misty moors and finds herself in a dystopian future, run by a cruel tyrant. She realises that somehow she has to change the past to prevent the future from happening. A gripping book with a twist in the storyline. **8–12**

BLACKMAN, MALORIE
Robot Girl

Barrington Stoke, 2015   ISBN: 9781781124598

Futuristic drama ideal for struggling readers. Claire's dad is working on something in his lab. When she finds out what it is she realises he's created a monster and now has to decide what to do about it. **8–12**

BRAHMACHARI, SITA
Tender Earth

Macmillan Children's Books, 2017   ISBN: 9781509812509

When Laila's older sisters leave home just as she starts secondary school, she has to adjust to not being the baby of the family any more. As she is trying to find her place in her new world, she rediscovers Nana Josie's Project Book with its messages of protest and finds her own voice to speak up for what she believes in. **8–12**

BRIDGES, SHIRIN YIM
Illustrated by Sophie Blackall

Ruby's Wish

Chronicle Books, 2015   ISBN: 9781452145693

Based on the true story of the author's grandmother. Ruby is a little girl who does not aspire to get married, like most of the other girls in China at the time, but is determined to attend university. Beautifully detailed illustrations bring a sense of place to this inspiring story about ambition and following your dreams. **8–12**

BUCKLEY, MICHAEL
Illustrated by Peter Ferguson

The Sisters Grimm: The Fairy-Tale Detectives

Amulet Books, 2017   ISBN: 9781419720055

In book one of the series, orphaned sisters, Sabrina and Daphne, are taken in by their grandmother where they discover they are descendants of the Brothers Grimm and next in a long line of fairy-tale detectives. There follows a collection of action-packed magical adventures involving various characters from well-known tales. **8–12**

BURTON, JESSIE

Illustrated by Angela Barrett

The Restless Girls

Bloomsbury, 2018   ISBN: 9781408886950

When Queen Laurelia dies in a car crash, the King decides that he must protect his twelve daughters at any cost. So he takes away their possessions and freedom. But the eldest, Princess Frida, will not give in so easily and uses her imagination to fight for the opportunity to live their lives freely. A feminist reinterpretation of the classic fairytale 'Twelve Dancing Princesses'. **8–12; 12–14**

CHILD, LAUREN

Ruby Redfort, Look into My Eyes

Harper Collins, 2015   ISBN: 9780007334070

Ruby is smart, independent and a genius, who can also stand up for herself, which is why Spectrum, a secret spy agency, has recruited her. A thrilling detective/spy story with a strong theme of friendship. **8–12; 12–14**

COOPER, ABBY

Sticks and Stones

Square Fish, 2017   ISBN: 9781250115263

Since she was a baby, people's thoughts about Elyse have appeared written on her skin. Now twelve years old, words like 'loser' and 'pathetic' are appearing and she's not sure how to deal with the way this makes her feel. A story about acceptance and self-confidence. **8–12**

COTTERILL, JO

Jelly

Piccadilly Press, 2018   ISBN: 9781848126732

Jelly is the class clown and perfect at mimicking her teachers. When people say unkind things to her, she is self-depreciating and just makes them laugh. However, her cheerful exterior hides an inner nature that is full of self-doubt with body image issues. Then her mum brings a new boyfriend home who is kind and understanding, and helps Jelly to believe in herself for who she is. **8–12**

DAHL, ROALD

Illustrated by Quentin Blake

Matilda

Puffin, 2016   ISBN: 9780141365466

Matilda is a magically gifted child who is also smart and intelligent but also totally misunderstood and ill-treated by her family. However, Miss Honey, her teacher, encourages her to develop her skills and stand up to the bullying adults in her life. A story about inner strength, determination and being who you are despite others wanting you to conform. **8–12**

DAVIES, LINDA
Longbow Girl
Chicken House, 2015   ISBN: 9781910002612

The De Courcys, owners of Black Castle, and the Owens, struggling farmers, have been enemies for years, fighting over their lands. When Merry Owen finds a buried chest full of ancient documents, it leads her back to a past filled with adventure, treasure and secrets. **8–12**

DEEN, SOPHIE and THORNTON, JOHN
Illustrated by Nathan Hackett
Detective Dot
Bright Little Labs, 2016   ISBN: 9780995636200

Detective Dot is a coder who works for the Children's Intelligence Agency (CIA) using technology and coding to bring down the evil teen, Shelly Belly. Full of fun, with interactive missions that enable readers to learn about coding, this book is informative and engages children with a range of environmental and ethical issues leading to further discussion. **8–12**

DENG, SALLY
Skyward: The Story of Female Pilots in World War Two
Flying Eye Books, 218   ISBN: 9781911171515

A fictionalised account based on the true story of three women pilots and their activities in World War Two. From the USA, England and Russia, they faced discrimination, sexism and inequality. **Under 8; 8–12**

DHAMI, NARINDER
13 Hours
Tamarind, 2015   ISBN: 9781848531161

Following an accident that left her with debilitating injuries, Anni's mother develops agoraphobia and anxiety, forcing Anni to become her carer. When a supposed terrorist group breaks into their attic, Anni finds an inner strength and determination to foil their plot. However, all is not what it seems and during the following thirteen hours, secrets are revealed that change lives forever. A pacy page-turning thriller. **8–12**

DICAMILLO, KATE
Raymie Nightingale
Walker Books, 2017   ISBN: 9781406373189

Raymie needs to win the Little Miss Central Florida tire competition so she'll get her photo in the newspaper, her dad will see it and return home. To win she has to compete with Louisiana, who has a show-biz background, and Beverly, who is determined to sabotage the contest. However, the three girls find themselves bonding and becoming friends, supporting each other in their very individual family situations. **8–12**

See also:
Louisiana's Way Home
Walker Books, 2018   ISBN: 9781406384208

Beverly, Right Here
Walker Books, 2019   ISBN: 9780763694647

DON, LARI

Illustrated by Francesca Greenwood

Girls, Goddesses and Giants

A&C Black, 2014   ISBN: 9781408188224

Folk tales from around the world featuring girls saving the day through courage, cunning and kindness. **8–12**

DRAPER, SHARON

Out of My Mind

Atheneum Books, 2016   ISBN: 9781416971719

Ten year old Melody has severe cerebral palsy and cannot speak so her teachers and classmates assume she is mentally as well as physically challenged. However, Melody is extremely smart, something she is determined to prove. An emotional book about a strong-willed little girl that will have you both crying with frustration and laughing with joy. **8–12**

DRIVER, SARAH

The Huntress Trilogy: Sea (Book 1)

Egmont, 2017   ISBN: 9781405284677

Mouse lives on the ocean with her grandma who is captain of 'The Huntress', a position Mouse will take over one day. Then Stag arrives, claiming her father is dead and taking over the ship. Mouse has to use her skills and bravery to rescue her father and claim back the ship. **8–12**

See also:

The Huntress: Sky (Book 2)

Egmont, 2017   ISBN: 9781405284684

The Huntress: Storm (Book 3)

Egmont, 2018   ISBN: 9781405284691

EDGE, CHRISTOPHER

12 Minutes to Midnight

Nosy Crow, 2012   ISBN: 9780857630506

When her father dies, Penelope Treadwell continues writing his magazine – 'The Penny Dreadful' – a publication full of macabre tales that is gripping Victorian Britain. When she finds herself caught up in mysterious events in Bedlam, an asylum for the mentally ill, Penny is plunged into a fast-paced yet terrifying adventure. **8–12**

EDGE, CHRISTOPHER

The Infinite Lives of Maisie Day

Nosy Crow, 2018   ISBN: 9781788000291

Maisie Day is a child prodigy and finds it difficult to make friends. When she wakes up on her birthday she discovers everyone has disappeared and a thick blackness covers everything. Can she find her family before it engulfs the house? A book that stretches the imagination. **8–12**

See also:

The Longest Night of Charlie Noon

Nosy Crow, 2019   ISBN: 9781788004947

GAIMAN, NEIL

Illustrated by Chris Riddell

Coraline

Bloomsbury Children's Books, 2013   ISBN: 9781408841754

Coraline is bold and curious so when she discovers an identical flat to hers through a door, it's natural for her to explore it. Everything seems better there except the 'other' mother and father want to keep her forever and Coraline has to fight, not only to save herself but also the other trapped souls. **8–12**

GINO, ALEX

George

Scholastic, 2017   ISBN: 9780545812573

People assume George is a boy because of the way she looks but she knows she is really a girl. When her teacher announces the class is going to perform 'Charlotte's Web', George is determined to play Charlotte but her teacher won't even let her try out for the part. However, George's best friend, Kelly, has a plan to get round this. A heartwarming tale about friendship and gender identity issues. **8–12**

HALE, SHANNON and HALE, DEAN

Illustrated by LeUyen Pham

The Princess in Black

Walker Books, 2017   ISBN: 9781406376456

The first book in a funny action-packed series about a princess who wears pink and turns into a superhero. When there's trouble, Princess Magnolia becomes the Princess in Black and in this book she's stopping the big blue monster from frightening the goats. Great story for showing that princesses can also be strong and resourceful. **Under 8**

See also:

The Princess in Black and the Perfect Princess Party

Walker Books, 2017   ISBN: 9781406376463

The Princess in Black and the Mysterious Playdate

Candlewick Press, 2018   ISBN: 9781536200515

HARGRAVE, KIRAN MILLWOOD

The Girl of Ink and Stars

Chicken House, 2016   ISBN: 978191002742

Isabella's father mapped faraway lands but she is forbidden to leave the island. When her friend disappears, Isabella is determined to find her, even if it means venturing into a wasteland filled with fire demons and monstrous wolves. A book about adventure, friendship and discovering yourself. **8–12; 12–14**

IRVING, ELLIE
The Matilda Effect

Corgi Childrens, 2017   ISBN: 9780552568371

Matilda loves science and inventing so is devastated when she doesn't win the school science fair, especially as the judges don't believe her idea is her own. She then discovers that her Grandma was also a scientist whose idea was stolen by somebody now about to get a Nobel Prize. Together they concoct a plan to tell everyone the truth. **8–12**

JARVIS, ROBIN
The Power of Dark (The Witching Legacy Book 1)

Egmont, 2016   ISBN: 9781405280235

Lil and Verne are best friends, living in the seaside town of Whitby, a place with an ancient curse that has been dormant for many years. The arrival of Mr Dark and his winged familiar revive the ancient powers, forcing Lil and Verne to join forces with Cherry Cerise, the last of the Whitby Witches, to save the town, and the people they know and love. **8–12**

KIERMAN, CELINE
Begone the Raggedy Witches (The Wild Magic Trilogy Book 1)

Walker Books, 2018   ISBN: 9781406366020

Mam is Mup's mother and heir to the Witches Borough, ruled over by the evil Queen, Mup's grandmother. Mam has rejected her heritage and is hiding out in our world. When she is discovered and foils a kidnap attempt by the witches, they steal Mup's father instead forcing Mam and Mup to cross the border to rescue him. A compelling and spooky magical story about power, friendship and responsibility. **8–12**

L'ENGLE, MADELEINE
A Wrinkle in Time

Puffin, 2014   ISBN: 9780141354934

A classic sci-fi fantasy adventure in which Charles, his sister Meg and friend Calvin go in search of his lost father through a 'wrinkle in time'. The story is dominated by the funny and mysterious trio of guardian angels known as Mrs Whatsit, Mrs Who and Mrs Which. **8–12**

LESTER, CAS
Do You Speak Chocolate?

Piccadilly Press, 2017   ISBN: 9781471405037

When Nadima joins Jaz's school after her family flee from Syria, they discover they share a love of music, dancing and chocolate. Jaz tries to help Nadima and her family but her plans backfire. A sensitive story about friendship, that explains the conflict in Syria and with a character who is determined to overcome dyslexia. **8–12**

McMULLEN, BETH
Mrs Smith's Spy School for Girls

Aladdin Books, 2017   ISBN: 9781481490214

Abigail is astonished when she discovers that, not only is her boarding school a cover for an elite spy ring, but that her mother is a top agent and has gone MIA. Cue a crash course in spy training and an adventure with a message about girl power. **8–12**

MORGAN, SALLY
My Best Friend, the Suffragette

Scholastic, 2018   ISBN: 9781407184623

Christine has been brought up to believe a woman's place is in the home; Mary has been taught that women can change the world. When the two meet they become friends but can their friendship survive the changes happening in society? Written in letter format, this story introduces ideas of prejudice, women in society and equality. **Under 8; 8–12**

NICHOLLS, SALLY

Illustrated by Hannah Coulson

All About Ella

Barrington Stoke, 2017   ISBN: 9781781125335

Ella is Sam's kid sister from the book *Ways to Live Forever*. Ella is fed up with Sam getting all the attention because he's ill but when he worsens, she realises that she's not really that bothered and actually cares about him very much. **Under 8**

PEREZ, CELIA C.
The First Rule of Punk

Puffin, 2018   ISBN: 9780425290422

Malu's first day at school doesn't go well but she is determined to follow her dad's code of 'always be yourself'. When she forms a band of like-minded punk misfits she finds herself up against the school administration who wants her to conform. But they haven't reckoned on her determination to stand up for the right to express herself. **8–12**

PIELICHATY, HELEN
GIRLS F.C. 1: Do Goalkeepers Wear Tiaras?

Walker Books, 2018   ISBN: 9781406383324

Nine year old Megan loves football and wants to be on the school team but is constantly ignored by the coach. Then she has an idea – to start her own all-girls team – but first she has to find ten other girls interested in playing football. **8–12**

POLACCO, PATRICIA
Bully

Putnam, 2012   ISBN: 9780399257049

Lyla is worried about starting at a new school but soon makes friends with Jamie. However, when she joins the cheerleading squad she finds herself mixing with a group of popular girls who tease and bully others online, including Jamie. Lyla decides she doesn't want to be part of the group so leaves them but they don't take kindly to what they see is a rejection of them. **8–12**

RIDDELL, CHRIS
Goth Girl and the Ghost of a Mouse

Macmillan Children's Books, 2017   ISBN: 9781447201744

Ada Goth is the only child of Lord Goth and is quite lonely living in Ghastly-Gorm Hall. When William and Emily Cabbage come to stay, they work together to foil the plot the dastardly gamekeeper is hatching.

Quirky and amusing, these books works on several levels, appealing to both younger readers and adults alike. Beautifully illustrated. **8–12**

See also:

Goth Girl and the Fete Worse Than Death

Macmillan, 2017   ISBN: 9780230759824

Goth Girl and the Wuthering Fright

Macmillan, 2017   ISBN: 9781447277897

Goth Girl and the Sinister Symphony

Macmillan, 2017   ISBN: 9781447277941

SKRYPUCH, MARSHA FORCHUK

Making Bombs for Hitler

Scholastic, 2019   ISBN: 9781338312836

Lida thinks she is safe because she's not Jewish but she is taken away from her parents and older sister, and sent to a work camp with other Ukrainian children. She is given the task of making bombs but has an idea – is she able to sabotage them and thus foil Hitler's plans? A novel about survival, courage and hope. **8- 12; 12–14**

SPINELLI, JERRY

The Warden's Daughter

Yearling, 2018   ISBN: 9780375832024

Cammie is the warden's daughter and lives at Hancock County prison, hanging out with the women in the exercise yard. But she misses her mum who died when she was a baby and the only place she's got to search for a new one is within the wall of Hancock. **8–12**

STEVENS, ROBIN

A Murder Most Unladylike

Puffin, 2016   ISBN: 9780141369761

Daisy Wells and Hazel Wong set up their own detective agency at Deepdean School for Girls but there's little to investigate until the Science Mistress, Miss Bell, is found dead in the gym. This is the first book in a series of crime mysteries featuring the two friends. **8–12**

STORR, CATHERINE

Illustrated by Marjorie-Ann Watts

Clever Polly and the Stupid Wolf

Puffin, 2015   ISBN: 9780141360232

Short stories about a wolf who wants to eat Polly, a little girl, who manages to talk or act her way out of every situation. A humorous book about being resourceful. **Under 8; 8–12**

TOWNSEND, JESSICA

Nevermore: The Trails of Morrigan Crow

Orion Children's Books, 2018   ISBN: 9781510103825

Morrigan Crow is destined to die on her eleventh birthday but at midnight on this fateful day, she is whisked away to the secret city of Nevermore where she is invited to join the Wondrous Society. However, first she has to pass four trials using powers she does not have. A magical adventure. **8–12**

See also:

Wundersmith: The Calling of Morrigan Crow

Orion Children's Books, 2018   ISBN: 9781510104440

WEBB, HOLLY

The Princess and the Suffragette

Scholastic, 2018   ISBN: 9781407185651

A sequel/spin-off the 'The Little Princess'. It is 1913. Lottie, the smallest girl from the original story, finds out about the Suffragettes and sneaks out to attend a demonstration in defiance of her father. An exciting adventure about female empowerment and friendship. **8–12**

WIENTGE, KRISTI

Karma Muller's Mustache

Simon & Schuster, 2018   ISBN: 9781481477710

Karma is mixed race, half Methodist and half Sikh, and if that wasn't enough to deal with, her best friend has found another best friend, her parents have swapped roles at home and she's being teased for having hairs growing on her upper lip. A story that tackles issues of self-esteem and body confidence. **8–12**

WILSON, JACQUELINE

Illustrated by Nick Sharratt

Opal Plumstead

Corgi, 2015   ISBN: 9780552574013

Set in the run-up to World War 1; when Opal's father is arrested for perjury, she is forced to leave school and work in a factory. There she finds friendship but is also bullied, and is introduced to the women's suffrage. **8–12**

WOLLARD, ELLI

Illustrated by Laura Ellen Anderson

Swashbuckle Lil: The Secret Pirate

Macmillan Children's Books, 2016   ISBN: 9781509808823

Nobody at school guesses Elli's secret, that she's really a pirate who needs to defeat the dreaded Stinkbeard and his crocodile to save sports day. **Under 8**

WYNNE JONES, DIANA

Howl's Moving Castle series

Harper Collins, 2010   ISBN: 9780007299263

After Sophie is turned into an old woman by the Witch of the Waste, she forms a pact with Michael, a wizard's apprentice, and Calcifer, a fire demon, to try and break the curse. A gripping and amusing story. **8–12**

Information Books

ADAMS, JULIA

Illustrated by Louise Wright

101 Awesome Women Who Changed Our World

Arcturus Publishing, 2018   ISBN: 9781788287111

A book about the inspirational stories of a wide range of women, from various nationalities and ages, covering the sciences, arts, exploration and activism. Each section includes biographies, quotations and facts about their achievements. **8–12**

AHMED, RODA

Illustrated by Stasia Burrington

Mae Among the Stars

HarperCollins, 2018   ISBN: 9780062651730

A picture book about the life of Dr Mae Jemison, the first African American woman to go into space. From a young child, Mae wanted to be an astronaut. Her curiosity, determination and intelligence helped make her dream come true. **Under 8.**

AMSON-BRADSHAW, GEORGIA

Illustrated by Rita Petruccioli

Brilliant Women: Amazing Artists and Designers

Wayland, 2018   ISBN: 9781438012179

Introducing women who have stretched the boundaries of art and design, and who have had a worldwide impact. Each story comes with an activity. **8–12**

See also:

Brilliant Women: Heroic Leaders and Activists

Wayland, 2018   ISBN: 9781438012186

Brilliant Women: Incredible Sporting Champions

Wayland, 2018   ISBN: 9781438012193

Brilliant Women: Pioneers of Science and Technology

Wayland, 2018   ISBN: 9781438012193

ANHOLT, LAURENCE

Frida Kahlo and the Bravest Girl In the World

Frances Lincoln Books, 2017   ISBN: 9781847806673

When Mariana goes to Frida's house to be painted, she learns about her life, and how creativity and courage can set you free. **Under 8**

ANHOLT, LAURENCE
Illustrated by Sheila Moxley

Stone Girl Bone Girl: The Story of Mary Anning of Lyme Regis

Frances Lincoln Books, 2006   ISBN: 9781845077006

The story of Mary Anning who found a fossilised sea monster as a child and went on to become a world-famous fossil hunter. **Under 8; 8–12**

APPLEBY, BEA and SPILSBURY, LOUISE

What Is Feminism? Why Do We Need it and Other Big Questions

Wayland, 2018   ISBN: 9780750298384

Divided into sections such as: Work and Money; Power and Politics; Media; Education; Family; and Bodies. This book looks at how feminism and the feminist movement have affected each area and the issues of today. **8–12**

APPS, ROY

Edge: Sporting Heroes – Fara Williams

Franklin Watts, 2018   ISBN: 9781445153292

The life story of Fara Williams, and how she became a world-class defender for Arsenal Ladies and an England regular. **8–12**

See also:

Edge: Sporting Heroes – Serena Williams

Franklin Watts, 2018   ISBN: 9781445153414

BAILEY, ELLEN; BEER, SOPHIE and FARNSWORTH, LAUREN

I Am a Wonder Woman

Buster Books, 2018   ISBN: 9781780555515

A look at the most inspirational women in history from ancient times to modern day. Activities and questions bring each story to life. **8–12**

BARNHAM, KAY

History VIPs: Emmeline Pankhurst

Wayland, 2016   ISBN: 9780750299404

Biography of Emmeline Pankhurst, from her early campaigns through to the granting of rights for women after the First World War. **8–12**

See also:

History VIPs: Mary Anning

Wayland, 2016   ISBN: 9780750299145

BEEVOR, LUCY

Illustrated by Sarah Green

Amazing Women: 101 Lives To Inspire You

Stripes Publishing, 2018   ISBN: 9781847159175

A collection of empowering and inspiring international female figures who have made significant contributions to society. As well as highlighting important historical figures, this book also features a range of contemporary and recognisable people. **8–12**

BRAMI, ELIZABETH

Illustrated by Estelle Billon-Spagnol

Declaration of the Rights of Girls

Little Island Books, 2017   ISBN: 9781910411278

The rights of girls to be who they want to be – dirty, messy, scruffy – and to do any job they want. Translated from French and endorsed by Amnesty International. **Under 8; 8–12**

BRIGHTON, CATHERINE

The Fossil Girl

Frances Lincoln Books, 2006   ISBN: 9781845077327

The true story of Mary Anning who found the first complete fossil of Ichthyosaurus, or fish lizard, when she was a child and became a famous fossil hunter. **Under 8**

BROWNLEE, LIZ; DEAN, JAN and MORGAN, MICHAELA

Reaching the Stars: Poems About Extraordinary Women and Girls

Macmillan Children's Books, 2017   ISBN: 9781509814282

A collection of poems celebrating the achievements of women and girls throughout history. **8–12 years**

CAVALLO, FRANCESCA and FAVILLI, ELENA

Illustrated by: Various

Goodnight Stories for Rebel Girls: 100 Tales of Extraordinary Women

Particular Books, 2017   ISBN: 9780120420476

A collection of one hundred stories about feminist role models. Each is a page long, so ideal for reading aloud or at bedtime, and is accompanied by an illustration of the person. These are stories about real women who have achieved incredible results, despite the odds, or whose actions, past and present, have changed history. **Under 8; 8–12**

See also:

Goodnight Stories for Rebel Girls 2

Timbuktu Labs, 2018   ISBN: 9780997895827

CLINTON, CHELSEA

Illustrated by: Alexandra Boiger

She Persisted: 13 American Women Who Changed the World

Philomel Books, 2017   ISBN: 9781524741723

Short, illustrated biographies on women who have spoken out for what's right, even when they have had to fight to be heard. These are stories of women who have shaped American history through their tenacity and persistence, sometimes through speaking out, sometimes by staying seated, sometimes by captivating an audience. **Under 8**

See also:

She Persisted: Around the World

Philomel Books, 2018   ISBN: 9780525516996

CLINE-RANSOME, LESA

Illustrated by James E. Ransome

Before She Was Harriet

Holiday House, 2017   ISBN: 9780823420476

Biography of Harriet Tubman, written in verse, detailing the many roles she had in her life: Union spy, slave and freedom fighter amongst them. **Under 8**

COLES, ROBERT

The Story of Ruby Bridges

Scholastic, 2010   ISBN: 9780439472265

The story of the first African American child to be integrated in a New Orleans school in 1960. **Under 8**

DELLACCIO, TANYA

Breakout Biographies: Emma Watson – Actress, Women's Rights Activist and Goodwill Ambassador

Powerkids Press, 2018   ISBN: 9781538326176

Best known for her role in Harry Potter as Hermione Granger, Watson is an advocate for women's rights and uses her fame to educate the world about these issues. **8–12**

DEPRINCE, MICHAELA

Illustrated by Ella Okstad

Ballerina Dreams: A True Story

Faber & Faber, 2017   ISBN: 9780571329731

Michaela was born in war-torn Sierra Leone. After her father was killed and her mother died, she was put in an orphanage where she was bullied. One day she found a magazine with a picture of a dancer on it which inspired her to learn ballet. Adopted and taken to live in America, this is the story of how Michaela overcame shyness and obstacles to live her dream. **Under 8**

DOYLE, CAITLYN

Illustrated by Chuck Gonzales

We Can Do Anything: 200 Incredible Women Who Changed the World

HarperCollins, 2018   ISBN: 9780008285616

Divided into topics including: Arts and Literature; Politics and World Building; Sports and Endurance; Business and Industry; and Science and Innovation. Each page contains biographical information and facts about a specific woman, written in accessible text and presented in chronological order. **8–12; 12–14**

FERTIG, DENNIS
Sylvia Earle: Ocean Explorer (Women In Conservation)

Raintree, 2015   ISBN: 9781406283433

The life and work of Sylvia Earle and her fight to protect the oceans, including her methods, findings and the impact of her work. **8–12**

FRANK, ANNE
The Diary of a Young Girl

Puffin, 2007   ISBN: 9780141315188

In July 1942, thirteen year old Anne and her family went into hiding in Amsterdam. Her diary describes her life and thoughts over the next two years until they were betrayed in August 1944. **8–12; 12–14**

GIFFORD, CLIVE
Inspirational Lives: Ellie Simmonds

Wayland, 2015   ISBN: 9780750283670

An introduction to the life and achievements of Ellie Simmonds, a Paralympian swimming champion. **8–12**

HALLIGAN, KATHERINE
Illustrated by Sarah Walsh

HerStory: 50 Women and Girls Who Shook the World

Nosy Crow Ltd, 2018   ISBN: 9781788001380

An inspiring book that celebrates the lives of fifty women and girls who defied challenges and barriers to make the world a better place, including leaders, artists, healers, teachers, scientists and mathematicians. Beautifully illustrated with facts, details and inspirational quotes. **Under 8, 8–12**

HANCOCKS, HELEN
Ella Queen of Jazz

Lincoln Children's Books, 2018   ISBN: 9781786031259

Ella was a singer who was on her way up until the biggest club in town refused to let her play because of her colour. Then Hollywood star, Marilyn Monroe, stepped in and the two formed a lasting friendship. **Under 8**

HARRISON, PAUL
History VIPs: Boudicca

Wayland, 201   ISBN: 9780750299176

A biography that looks at the life of Boudicca, who shaped the course of history by leading a rebellion against Roman rule in Britain. **8–12**

HARRISON, VASHTI
Little Leaders: Bold Women in Black History

Puffin, 2018   ISBN: 9780241346839

Informative and empowering, the stories of forty inspiring black women who broke barriers. **Under 8; 8–12**

See also:

Little Leaders: Visionary Women Around the World

Puffin, 2018   ISBN: 9780241346877

HERNANDEZ, LAURIE
I Got This: To Gold and Beyond

HarperCollins, 2018   ISBN: 9780062677326

In 2016, Hernandez was chosen to be part of the US Olympic gymnastics team, winning a gold medal as part of the Final Five and an individual silver medal. This is her story about growing up with her dream, her training, sacrifices and triumphs. **8–12**

HOOD, SUSAN
Illustrated by Sophie Blackall et al

Shaking Things Up: 14 Young Women Who Changed the World

HarperCollins, 2018   ISBN: 9780062699459

A poetry book that introduces fourteen young women who changed the world; some well-known names, others not so famous. Each poem is illustrated by a different artist. **Under 8**

HOWELL, IZZI
Fact Cat: History – Mary Seacole

Wayland, 2017   ISBN: 9781526303677

An introduction to the life and work of Mary Seacole, how she learned about herbal medicine and helped soldiers in the Crimean War. **Under 8**

HUDSON, WADE and HUDSON, CHERYL WILLIS
We Rise, We Resist, We Raise Our Voices

Pisces Books, 2018   ISBN: 9780525580423

An anthology of fifty culturally diverse voices. Original art and prose from children's authors and illustrators giving words of inspiration and hope to young activists. **8–12**

IGNOTOFSKY, RACHEL
Women in Sport: Fifty Fearless Athletes Who Played to Win

Wren & Rook, 2018   ISBN: 9781526360922

Celebrating the success of women who paved the way for today's athletes including well-known figures like tennis player Serena Williams and broadcaster Clare Balding, as well as lesser-known pioneers like Gertrude Ederle, the first woman to swim the English Channel, and Keiko Fukuda, the highest-ranked female judoka in history. **8–12**

See also:

Women in Science: Fifty Fearless Pioneers Who Changed the World

Wren & Rook, 2017   ISBN: 9781526360519

JACKSON, LIBBY

A Galaxy of Her Own: Amazing Stories of Women in Space

Century, 2017   ISBN: 9781780898360

Fifty stories from around the world about women who have been crucial to the story of space exploration; from Ada Lovelace in the 19th century to astronauts on the International Space Station. Illustrated by artwork from students of the London College of Communication. **Under 8; 8–12**

KAISER, LISBETH

Illustrated by Marta Antelo

Little People, Big Dreams: Rosa Parks

Frances Lincoln Books, 2017   ISBN: 9781786030184

Rosa grew up during segregation in Alabama. When she refused to give up her seat on the bus to a white man, it sparked a bus boycott and had a huge impact on civil rights. With information about Rosa's life as a child to appeal to younger readers, quirky illustrations and additional facts. **Under 8**

See also:

Little People Big Dreams: Maya Angelou

Illustrated by Leire Salaberria

Lincoln Children's Books, 2016   ISBN: 9781847808905

Little People, Big Dreams: Emmeline Pankhurst

Illustrated by Ana Sanfelippo

Frances Lincoln, 2017   ISBN: 9781786030207

KEATING, JESS

Illustrated by Marta Alvarez Miguens

Shark Lady: The Daring Tale of How Eugenie Clark Dove into History

Sourcebooks, 2017   ISBN: 9781492642046

Eugenie Clark fell in love with sharks when she was a young child but soon discovered that not everyone felt the way she did about them. She also learnt that people did not think women should be scientists. Eugenie grew up to prove them wrong by becoming the world famous 'Shark Lady'. **Under 8**

LAWLOR, LAURIE

Super Women: Six Scientists Who Changed the World

Holiday House, 2019   ISBN: 9780823441860

Biographical profiles of six women who, through ambition and perseverance, broke new ground with their research in STEM subjects. Featuring Katherine Coleman Johnson, mathematician; Eugenie Clark, ichthyologist; Marie Tharp, cartographer; Florence Hawley Ellis, anthropologist; Gertrude Elion, pharmacologist; and Margaret Burbridge, astrophysicist. **8–12; 12–14**

LEVY, DEBBIE
Illustrated by Elizabeth Baddeley

I Dissent: Ruth Bader Ginsburg Makes Her Mark

Simon & Schuster, 2018   ISBN: 9781481465595

A picture book about the life of Supreme Court Justice, Ruth Bader Ginsburg, who has spent her life fighting for gender equality and civil justice. **Under 8; 8–12**

MACY, SUE
Illustrated by Matt Collins

Trudy's Big Swim: How Gertrude Ederle Swam the English Channel and Took the World by Storm

Holiday House, 2017   ISBN: 9780823436651

The story of how Gertrude Ederle became the first woman to swim across the English Channel in 1926. With a timeline and source notes, this biography is set against a background of previous successful and failed attempts, as well as how athletics was gaining in popularity at the time. **Under 8**

MAGGS, SAM
Illustrated by Jenn Woodall

Girl Squads: 20 Female Friendships That Changed History

Quirk Books, 2018   ISBN: 9781683690726

Inspiring and diverse, this book details a range of profiles of some of history's most influential women spanning the arts, science, activism and sport. Fun and informative, it focuses on groups of women rather than individuals. **8–12**

MARTIN, CLAUDIA

Inspirational Lives: Malala Yousafzai

Wayland, 2016   ISBN: 9780750293143

Discover how Malala stood up to the Taliban in defending her right to an education. The inspiring story of the youngest-ever Nobel Prize laureate. **8–12**

McCANN, MICHELLE ROEHM and WELDEN, AMELIE

Girls Who Rocked the World

Simon & Schuster, 2017   ISBN: 9781471171017

This book features forty-six young women from across history and around the world who have all achieved remarkable things as teenagers (or younger). Historical figures as well as contemporary examples are covered. **8–12**

McDONNELL, PATRICK

Me... Jane

Little, Brown Books for Young Readers, 2019   ISBN: 9780316045469

Picture book aimed at younger readers that tells the story of the young Jane Goodall and her childhood toy chimpanzee that inspired her to live a life 'with and helping all animals'. With anecdotes taken from Jane Goodall's autobiography. **Under 8**

MELTZER, BRAD
Illustrated by Christopher Eliopoulos

I Am Sacagawea (Ordinary People Change the World)
Dial Books, 2017   ISBN: 9780525428534

The story of the only girl to accompany Lewis and Clark on their exploration of the Mississippi River in the 1800s, Sacagawea was also the only Native American in the party. She acted as their communicator and carried her baby with her on her back the whole journey. **Under 8**

See also:

I Am Amelia Earhart
Dial Books, 2014   ISBN: 9780803740822

I Am Rosa Parks
Dial Books, 2014   ISBN: 9780803740853

I Am Jane Goodall
Dial Books, 2016   ISBN: 9780525428497

I Am Harriet Tubman
Dial Books, 2018   ISBN: 9780735228719

MOSCA, JULIA FINLEY
Illustrated by Daniel Rieley

Amazing Scientists: The Doctor with an Eye for Eyes: The Story of Patricia Bath
The Innovation Press, 2017   ISBN: 9781943147311

Growing up during the Civil rights Movement, Patricia Bath was determined to be a doctor. Overcoming racism, poverty and sexism, she achieved her dream and was responsible for an important treatment for blindness. **Under 8**

See also:

The Girl Who Thought in Pictures: The Story of Dr Temple Grandin
The Innovation Press, 2017   ISBN: 9781943147304

The Girl with a Mind for Math: The Story of Raye Montague
The Innovation Press, 2018   ISBN: 9781943147427

MURPHY, ADAM and MURPHY, LISA
Corpse Talk: Ground Breaking Women
David Fickling Books, 2018   ISBN: 9781910989609

Interviews with dead famous women who changed the world. Fascinating, funny and informative. **8–12**

NAPOLI, DONNA JO
Illustrated by Kadir Nelson

Mamma Miti
Simon & Schuster, 2017   ISBN: 9781416935056

The life of Wangari Maathia, the first African woman to win the Nobel Peace prize for her work in planting forests in Kenya and creating the Green Belt Movement, dedicated to sustainable development. **Under 8**

PANKHURST, KATE
Fantastically Great Women Who Changed the World

Bloomsbury Children's Books, 2016   ISBN: 9781408876985

An informative books containing facts about and achievements by a wide range of women. Colourfully illustrated. **Under 8**

See also:

Fantastically Great Women Who Made History

Bloomsbury Children's Books, 2018   ISBN: 9781408878897

Fantastically Great Women Who Worked Wonders

Bloomsbury Children's Books, 2019   ISBN: 9781408899274

PATERSON, KATHERINE
My Brigadista Year

Walker Books, 2018   ISBN: 9781406380811

The story of how thirteen year old Lora joined Premier Castro's army of literacy teachers and played her part in the struggle to teach fellow Cubans how to read and write. **8–12; 12–14**

RIDDLES, LIBBY
Illustrated by Shannon Cartwright

Storm Run: The Story of the First Woman to Win the Iditarod Dog Sled Race

Little Bigfoot, 2002   ISBN: 9781570612930

In 1985, Libby Riddles made history by becoming the first woman to win the 1,100-mile Iditarod Sled Dog Race. This autobiographical adventure story details all aspects of the race, together with photographs and illustrations. A compelling account of arctic storms, freezing temperatures, loyal sled dogs, and utter determination. **Under 8; 8–12**

RIDLEY, SARAH
Suffragettes and the Fight for the Vote

Franklin Watts, 2019   ISBN: 9781445152615

This book uses fourteen objects to tell the story of women's fight to get the vote in Britain. It looks at the role of women from the nineteenth century through to the struggle for equal rights today. **8–12**

ROBBINS, DEAN
Illustrated by Lucy Knisley

Margaret and the Moon: How Margaret Hamilton Saved the First Lunar Landing

Knoff Books for Young Readers, 2017   ISBN: 9780399551857

A true story from one of the women of NASA that details how mathematician, Margaret Hamilton, hand-wrote the computer code that enabled the success of the Apollo spaceship missions. **Under 8, 8–12**

ROBINSON, FIONA

Ada's Idea: The Story of Ada Lovelace, the World's First Computer Programmer

Abrams Books, 2016   ISBN: 9781419718724

When Ada's parents separated her mother, a mathematician, insisted on a logic-focused education although Ada was always fascinated by her father's writing. Via her friendship with Charles Babbage, she became involved in programming his Analytical Engine, the precursor to the computer. A picture book biography. **Under 8**

SAMPSON, ANA

She Is Fierce: Brave, Bold and Beautiful Poems by Women

Macmillan Children's Books, 2018   ISBN: 9781509899425

One hundred and fifty poems from culturally diverse women writers, featuring well-known classics as well as contemporary voices. With short biographies on each poet, this book is divided into sections, for example, friendship, freedom and endings. **8–12; 12–14**

SAUJANI, RESHMA

Girls Who Code: Learn to Code and Change the World

Virgin Books, 2017   ISBN: 9780753557600

Written by the founder of the 'Girls Who Code' organisation, this book is an excellent introduction to coding, with an explanation of the principles as well as real-life stories about women who code. There are also details of linked careers as well as the use of coding in everyday life. **8–12**

SCHATZ, KATE

Illustrated by Miriam Klein Stahl

Rad Women Worldwide

Ten Speed Press, 2016   ISBN: 9780399578861

Biographical profiles of a diverse collection of forty women from 430BCE to 2016, covering a world-wide geographical spread of thirty-one countries. There is also a comprehensive list of additional names for further research. **8–12**

See also:

Rad Girls Can (Rad Women)

Ten Speed Press, 2018   ISBN: 9780399581106

SHEN, ANN

Bad Girls Throughout History: 100 Remarkable Women Who Changed the World

Chronicle Books, 2016   ISBN: 9781452153933

With striking watercolour portraits, this book features 100 revolutionary women who challenged the status quo and changed the rules, from pirates and artists to warriors and scientists. **8–12; 12–14**

See also:

Legendary Ladies: 50 Goddesses to Empower and Inspire You

Chronicle Books, 2018   ISBN: 9781452163413

SKEERS, KINDA

Illustrated by Livi Gosling

Women Who Dared: 52 Fearless Daredevils, Adventurers and Rebels

Sourcebooks Jabberwocky, 2017   ISBN: 9781492653271

Women have been doing incredible things for years and have mainly been ignored by history books. This compilation of biographies features an amazing array of women who will inspire others to explore, travel and discover. **8–12: 12–14**

SMITH, MATTHEW CLARK

Illustrated by Matt Tavares

Lighter Than Air

Candlewick Press, 2017   ISBN: 9780763677329

In eighteenth century France, ballooning was a new craze, despite the fact it was very dangerous. Records were being broken by aeronauts but they were all men. Sophie Blanchard's dream was to fly and she became the first woman to fly in a balloon on her own. A picture book biography. **8–12**

STEWART, LOUISE KAY

Illustrated by Eve Lloyd Knight

Rebel Voices: The Rise of Votes for Women

Wren & Rook, 2018   ISBN: 9781526300232

A compendium of stories about women from around the world who campaigned globally for equal rights. Commencing in New Zealand at the end of the 19th century and continuing up to the present day. **8–12**

THOMAS, ISABEL

Illustrated by Anke Weckmann

Little Guides to Great Lives: Marie Curie

Laurence King Publishing, 2018   ISBN: 9781786271525

Small format biographies that introduce children to inspirational women. Starting with their childhood, these are informative and entertaining, containing fascinating details about the subjects' lives. **8–12**

See also:

Little Guides to Great Lives: Amelia Earhart

Illustrated by Dahlia Adillon

Laurence King Publishing, 2018   ISBN: 9781786271594

Little Guides to Great Lives: Frida Kahlo

Illustrated by Marianne Madriz

Laurence King Publishing, 2018   ISBN: 9781786272997

VALDEZ, PATRICIA

Illustrated by Felicita Sala

Joan Procter, Dragon Doctor: The Woman Who Loved Reptiles

Andersen Press, 2018   ISBN: 9781783447411

A picture book biography about a female scientist who loved reptiles and became the curator of reptiles at the British Museum as well as designing the reptile house at the London Zoo. Colourful pictures illustrate an inspiring story about a fascinating woman who followed her dreams. **Under 8**

VAN ALLSBURG, CHRIS
Queen of the Falls

Andersen Press, 2019   ISBN: 9781849392860

Set in America in 1901, this is the true story of 62 year old Annie Taylor who decided to seek fame and fortune rather than go into the Poor House, by going over Niagara Falls in a wooden barrel. A rather intriguing tale about a strong and feisty woman. **8–12**

VEGARA, ISABELLA SANCHEZ

Illustrated by Maria Diamantes

Little People Big Dreams: Jane Austen

Lincoln Children's Books, 2018   ISBN: 9781786031198

A series of books that explores the lives of outstanding women, from scientists to artists to activists. They all began life as a child with a dream but through their determination and strong-will went on to achieve amazing things, often in difficult circumstances. **Under 8**

See also:

Little People Big Dreams: Marie Curie

Illustrated by Katie Wilson

Lincoln Children's Books, 2017   ISBN: 9781847809612

Little People Big Dreams: Simone de Beauvoir

Illustrated by Christine Roussey

Lincoln Children's Books, 2108   ISBN: 9781786032935

Little People Big Dreams: Amelia Earhart

Illustrated by Frau Isa

Lincoln Children's Books, 2016   ISBN: 9781847808851

Little People Big Dreams: Ella Fitzgerald

Illustrated by Barbara Alca

Lincoln Children's Books, 2018   ISBN: 9781786030863

Little People Big Dreams: Audrey Hepburn

Illustrated by Amaia Arrazola

Lincoln Children's Books, 2017   ISBN: 9781786030528

Little People Big Dreams: Maria Montessori

Illustrated by Raquel Martin

Lincoln Children's Books, 2019   ISBN: 9781786037534

Little People Big Dreams: Dolly Parton

Illustrated by Daria Solak

Lincoln Children's Books, 2019   ISBN: 9781786037596

Little People Big Dreams: Harriet Tubman

Illustrated by Pili Aguado

Lincoln Children's Book, 2018   ISBN: 9781786032898

Little People Big Dreams: Vivienne Westwood

Illustrated by Laura Callaghan

Lincoln Children's Books, 2019   ISBN: 9781786037565

WALLMARK, LAURIE

Illustrated by Katy Wu

Women Who Changed Our World: Grace Hopper – Queen of Computer Code

Sterling, 2017   ISBN: 9781454920007

Grace Hopper was a little girl who had a passion for maths, science and technology. She grew up, became a computer programmer and changed the world of computer science. **Under 8**

WILLIAMS, MARCIA

Three Cheers for Women

Walker Books, 2017   ISBN: 9781406374865

A celebration of the discoveries and achievements of over seventy inspirational women from all over the world and throughout history. Told in comic-book format, with facts, quotes, jokes and lots of attention to detail in the illustrations. **8–12**

WINTER, JEANETTE

Wangari's Trees of Peace

HMH Books for Young Readers, 2018ISBN: 9781328869210

Picture book biography that tells the story of Wangari who was an environmentalist and won the Nobel Peace Prize. Growing up in Kenya, Wangari was shocked when she returned to the country to discover the decimation of tress that had occurred. She started planting seedlings to replace them and from this idea grew a plan to fight for the environment. **Under 8**

WINTER, JONAH

Illustrated by Stacy Innerst

Ruth Bader Ginsburg: The Case of Ruth Bader Ginsburg vs Inequality

The inspirational story of Ruth Bader Ginsberg, daughter of Jewish migrants who fled persecution in Europe, known for her support for civil and women's rights. After training as a lawyer, Ruth became only the second woman to serve as a Supreme Court Justice in the USA. **Under 8**

YOUSAFZAI, MALALA

Illustrated by Kerascoet

Malala's Magic Pencil

Puffin, 2017   ISBN: 9780241322567

As a child, Malala wished for a magic pencil that would redraw reality. She never got her pencil but by working hard was able to make her wishes come true. An illustrated book that tells Malala's story in her own words for younger children. **Under 8; 8–12**

Graphic Novels and Manga

ARNI, SAMHITA

Illustrated by Moyna Chitrakar

Sita's Ramayana

Tara Books, 2012   ISBN: 9789380340036

This story brings a woman's perspective to the tale of the Ramayana – an heroic war in which Sita endures her fate until she decides to challenge it. Exploring the ideas of right and wrong, loyalty and trust, this Hindu story has influenced Indian culture over the centuries. **8–12; 12–14**

BASTIAN, JEREMY

The Cursed Pirate Girl

Boom Entertainment, 2016   ISBN: 9781608868339

A surreal fantasy adventure that involves the cursed pirate girl going on a quest in search of her father. Encountering mythical creatures, ancient pirates and ghostly apparitions, her adventures take her both across and below the seas. **8–12; 12–14**

BELL, CECE
El Deafo

Amulet Books, 2014   ISBN: 9781419712173

A memoir written in graphic format that details the author's experiences of hearing loss at a young age and how she got to grips with her hearing aid which was not always successful. Inspiring, compelling and funny, this is a very personal story of how one girl overcame her disabilities. **8–12**

BENDIS, BRIAN MICHAEL

Illustrated by Michael Avon Oeming

Takio

Marvel, 2011   ISBN: 9780785153269

Two sisters in a multi-racial family who don't get on but their over-protective mother makes them do everything together. When an accident results in them having super powers, they have to work together to save the world … and be home by 6! **8–12; 12–14**

BURKS, JAMES
Gabby and Gator

Yen Press, 2015   ISBN: 9780316259354

Gator's habit of eating the other pets has meant he's never really fitted in. Gabby has never fitted in either – she'd rather play her tuba than hang around the pool with the other girls. Then Gabby and Gator meet and discover that real friends accept you as you are. **Under 8; 8–12**

CAMERON, NEILL

Illustrated by Kate Brown

Tamsin and the Deep

David Fickling Books, 2016   ISBN: 9781910200773

After Tamsin is wiped out on her surfboard, she is dragged down to the deep – and into a world of mermaid magic where she discovers that her family are in danger and she is the only one who can save them. **Under 8; 8–12**

CAMERON, NEILL and HARTWELL, DAN

Pirates of Pangaea

David Fickling Books, 2015   ISBN: 9781910200087

The island of Pangaea, where dinosaurs still roam, is the most dangerous place on earth. Sophie Delacourt is sent there to stay with her uncle but is kidnapped by pirates. Can she escape and find her way safely home? **8–12**

CASTELLUCCI, CECIL

Illustrated by Jose Pimienta

Soupy Leaves Home

Dark Horse, 2017   ISBN: 9781616554312

Pearl aka Soupy runs away after an argument with her father and disguises herself as a boy. She meets Ramshackle, a hobo, who takes her under his wing. Set in 1932, this is a story about two misfits whose friendship helps both of them to heal their wounds. **8–12**

CHANANI, NIDHI

Pashmina

First Second, 2017   ISBN: 9781626720879

Priyanka Das has lots of questions about her Indian heritage but as far as her mother is concerned, that part of her life is closed. When Priyanka finds a pashmina in a suitcase and puts it on, she is mysteriously transported to India but is it real or something conjured by wishful thinking? A magical realism adventure. **8–12**

DEUTSCH, BARRY

Hereville: How Mirka Got Her Sword

Abrams, 2010   ISBN: 9781419706196

A fantasy about an eleven year old Jewish girl who lives in a strict Orthodox community and whose life is filled with school work, chores and rules. However, she is determined to find a sword and kill monsters! **8–12**

ESPINOSA, ROD

The Courageous Princess: Beyond the Hundred Kingdoms (Volume 1)

Dark Horse, 2015   ISBN: 9781616557225

Princess Mabelrose fights dragons, trolls and other creatures with bravery, intelligence and the help of her friends. A fantasy world of danger and adventure. **8–12, 12–14**

See also:

Volume 2: The Unremembered Lands

Dark Horse, 2015   ISBN: 9781616557232

Volume 3: The Dragon Queen

Dark Horse, 2015   ISBN: 9781616557249

FRANK, ANNE

Illustrated by David Polonsky

Adapted by Ari Folman

Anne Frank's Diary: The Graphic Adaptation

Pantheon Books, 2018   ISBN: 9781101871799

Authorised by the Anne Frank Foundation, this is a graphic novel adaptation of Anne Frank's diary that provides a good starting point for younger readers. Includes direct quotes from the diary and maintains the integrity of the original work. **8–12; 12–14**

GAIMAN, NEIL

Illustrated by Craig P. Russell

Coraline: The Graphic Novel

Bloomsbury, 2008   ISBN: 9780747594062

Coraline is bold and curious so when she discovers an identical flat to hers through a door, it's natural for her to explore it. Everything seems better there except the 'other' mother and father want to keep her forever and Coraline has to fight, not only to save herself but also the other trapped souls. **8–12**

GOWNLEE, JIMMY

Amelia Rules: The Whole World's Crazy

Atheneum Books, 2009   ISBN: 9781416986041

Amelia is nine years old and has moved from New York to a small town. She deals with bullying and surviving gym class with the help of her mum, her ex-rock star aunt and her friends. **8–12**

See also:

When the Past Is a Present

Atheneum Books, 2010   ISBN: 9781416986072

The Tweenage Guide to Not Being Unpopular

Atheneum Books, 2010   ISBN: 9781416986089

HALE, SHANNON

Illustrated by LeUyen Pham

Real Friends

First Second, 2017   ISBN: 9781626727854

A graphic memoir that tackles the issues of friendship, bullying and fitting in. Honest and heartfelt, this is an insightful look at growing up. **8–12**

HATKE, BEN
Little Robot

First Second, 2015   ISBN: 9781626720800

When a lonely girl finds a robot in the woods, she accidentally activates him and finally has a friend. But the big bad robots are after him and it's up to his new friend to save him. **Under 8**

HATKE, BEN
Zita the Spacegirl

First Second, 2011   ISBN: 9781596434462

When Zita's best friend is abducted by an alien, she rushes off to rescue him but finds herself in the middle of an intergalactic adventure. Zita has to discover where he's been hidden before the planet gets hit by an asteroid. **8–12**

See also:

Legends of Zita the Spacegirl

First Second, 2012   ISBN: 9781596434479

Return of Zita the Spacegirl

First Second, 2014   ISBN: 9781596438767

JAMIESON, VICTORIA
Roller Girl

Puffin Books, 2017   ISBN: 9780141378992

Astrid and Nicole are best friends and do everything together. However, when Astrid signs up for roller camp, Nicole decides she'd rather go to ballet camp. This makes it a difficult summer for Astrid as she explores who she is without Nicole by her side whilst trying to become the roller derby winner. **8–12**

KROSOCZKA, JARRETT J.
Lunch Lady and the Cyborg Substitute

Alfred A Knopf Books, 2009   ISBN: 9780375846830

Hector, Terrance and Dee aren't sure about their lunch lady and wonder what she does when she's not serving them. Little do they know that she has a secret hideout full of gadgets that she uses to fight crime and injustice. Quirky fun. **Under 8; 8–12**

LAWRENCE, MIKE
Star Scouts

First Second, 2017   ISBN: 9781626722804

Everyone thinks Arani is weird because she's not into make-up and boys like the rest of her Flower Scout group. When she's abducted by an alien Star Scout she fits right in – she just has to stop her dad realising she's off having fun and adventures around the universe. **8–12**

See also:

Star Scouts: The League of Lasers

First Second, 2018   ISBN: 9781626722811

NAIFEH, TED
Polly and the Pirates

Oni Press, 2006   ISBN: 9781932664461

Polly's mother was the daughter of a famous pirate queen. When her old crew kidnap Polly, she finds herself in the middle of an adventure centred around a treasure map that is wanted by the son of a pirate king. An action story with engaging characters, about standing up for your friends. **8–12**

See also:

Mystery of the Dragon Fish

Oni Press, 2012   ISBN: 9781934964736

ORCHARD, ERIC
Bera the One-Headed Troll

First Second, 2016   ISBN: 9781626721067

A human baby arrives in the land of the trolls and everyone wants to kill it except for Bera who decides it needs to be reunited with its parents. A spooky fantasy adventure. **8–12**

PEARSON, LUKE
Hilda and the Troll

Flying Eye Books, 2015   ISBN: 9781909263789

Blue-haired Hilda is an adventurous little girl with an inquisitive nature. One day, whilst out exploring the mountains, she gets lost in a sandstorm, spots a troll, befriends a wooden man and almost gets squashed by a giant! An exciting story full of magical wonder. **8–12**

See also:

Hilda and the Bird Parade

Flying Eye Books, 2016   ISBN: 9781911171027

Hilda and the Black Hound

Flying Eye Books, 2017   ISBN: 9781911171072

REEDER, AMY and MONTCLARE, BRANDON
Illustrated by Natacha Bustos

Moon Girl and Devil Dinosaur Volume 1: BFF

Marvel, 2016   ISBN: 9781302900052

Lunella Lafayette is a super genius with dormant inhuman genes. She wants to change the world but ends up opening a time portal that lets through a Devil Dinosaur as well as Killer Folk. Accepting her inheritance, she befriends D Dino and together they set out to defeat the Killer Folk. **8–12**

See also:

Moon Girl Volume 2: Moon Girl and the Cosmic Cooties

Marvel, 2017   ISBN: 9781302902087

Moon Girl Volume 3: The Smartest There Is

Marvel, 2017   ISBN: 9781302905347

SIEGEL, SIENA CHERSON
Illustrated by Mark Siegel

To Dance: A Ballerina's Graphic Novel

Atheneum Books, 2006   ISBN: 9781416926870

An autobiography of Siena's journey from Puerto Rico to her debut performance with the New York City Ballet. Also contains ballet facts. **8–12; 12–14**

TAKEUCHI, NAOKO
Sailor Moon

Kodansha Comics, 2018   ISBN: 9781632361523

When Usagi Tsukino adopts a stray cat, she discovers it is a talking cat called luna who informs her she is the Sailor Moon, a magical princess from the future whose mission is to protect the Solar Sytem. Book 1 in the series. **8–12; 12–14**

TELGEMEUR, RAINA
Smile

Scholastic, 2010   ISBN: 9780545132060

When Raina trips and damages her teeth, she has to wear braces and a head retainer. This leads to her being teased by her friends and losing self-confidence. However, she realises the best thing she can do is find new friends who accept her for who she is. **8–12; 12–14**

See also:

Sisters

Scholastic, 2014   ISBN: 9780545540605

WEBSTER, CHRISTY
Illustrated by Erik Doescher

Brave Batgirl!

Random House, 2017   ISBN: 9781524717117

A great introduction to the iconic superhero for younger readers. It used basic vocabulary and short sentences so is perfect for emerging readers. **Under 8**

WILLIAMSON, JOSHUA
Illustrated by Vicente Navarrete

Sketch Monsters: Escape of the Scribbles

Oni Press, 2011   ISBN: 9781934964699

Eight year old Mandy doesn't show her emotions but instead draws them in the form of monsters in her sketchbook. One day they escape and she has to catch them before they destroy the town. A unique way to help children express their emotions. **Under 8: 8–12**

YEE, LISA

Illustrated by Random House

Wonder Woman at Super Hero High

Puffin, 2016   ISBN: 9780141374734

Book 1 in the *Super Hero Girls* series. Wonder Woman wants to be the best at Super-Hero High School but there's a lot she has to get used to, including the fact that somebody doesn't want her there. **8–12**

YOLEN, JANE

Illustrated by Mike Cavallaro

Foiled

First Second, 2010   ISBN: 9781596432796

Alliera Carstairs is centre stage at the fencing studio but doesn't fit in at school. Although colour blind, she suddenly sees the world of colour whilst wearing her fencing mask; however, this also includes seeing fairies, dragons and demons. **8–12; 12–14**

See also:

Curses! Foiled Again

First Second, 2013   ISBN: 9781596436190

YOLEN, JANE

The Last Dragon

Dark Horse, 2016   ISBN: 9781616558741

Years ago humans drove the dragons from the Islands of May. Now they have returned to reclaim their land and only a healer's daughter stands in their way. **8–12**

Index of Authors

Ace, Lauren 9
Adams, Julia 28
Ahmed, Roda 28
Amson-Bradshaw, Georgia 28
Anholt, Lawrence 28,29
Appleby, Bea 29
Apps, Roy 29
Arni, Samhita 42
Atinuke 18
Bailey, Ellen 29
Barnham, Kay 29
Barnhill, Kelly 18
Bastian, Jeremy 42
Beaty, Andrea 9
Becker, Aaron 9
Beer, Sophie 29
Beevor, Lucy 30
Bell, Alex 18
Bell, Cece 42
Bendis, Brian Michael 42
Benjamin, Floella 9
Blackman, Malorie 18,19
Brahmachari, Sita 19
Brami, Elizabeth 30
Bridges, Shirin Yim 19
Brighton, Catherine 30
Brownlee, Liz 30
Bryan, Jason 10
Bryan, Kerrine 10
Buckley, Michael 19
Burks, James 42
Burton, Jessie 20
Cameron, Neill 43
Castellucci, Cecil 43
Cavallo, Francesca 30
Chanani, Nidhi 43
Child, Lauren 20
Cline-Ransome, Lesa 31
Clinton, Chelsea 30,31
Coelho, Joseph 10
Cole, Babette 10
Coles, Robert 31
Cooper, Abby 20
Cordell, Matthew 10
Cotterill, Jo 20
Cowell, Cressida 10
Dahl, Roald 20
Davies, Linda 21
Dean, Jan 30
Deen, Sophie 21
Dellaccio, Tanya 31

Deng, Sally 21
Deprince, Michaela 31
Deutsch, Barry 43
Dhami, Narinder 21
Dicamillo, Kate 21
Docherty, Helen 11
Docherty, Thomas 11
Don, Lari 22
Donaldson, Julia 11
Doyle, Caitlyn 31
Draper, Sharon 22
Driver, Sarah 22
Edge, Christopher 22
Epinosa, Rod 43,44
Falconer, Ian 11
Farnsworth, Lauren 29
Favilli, Elena 30
Fertig, Dennis 32
Folman, Ari (Translator) 44
Foreman, Michael 11
Frank, Anne 32,44
Funke, Cornelia 11
Gaiman, Neil 23,44
Garza, Lucinda Leonor 12
Gifford, Clive 32
Gino, Alex 23
Goodhart, Pippa 12
Gownlee, Jimmy 44
Hale, Dean 23
Hale, Shannon 23,44
Hargrave, Kiran Millwood 23
Halligan, Katherine 32
Hancocks, Helen 32
Harrison, Paul 32
Harrison, Vashti 32,33
Hart, Caryl 12
Hartwell, Dan 43
Hatke, Ben 44
Hernandez, Laurie 33
Hoffman, Mary 12
Hood, Susan 33
Howarth, Naomi 13
Howell, Izzi 33
Hudson, Cheryl Willis 33
Hudson, Wade 33
Irving, Ellie 24
Ismail, Yasmeen 13
Ignotofsky, Rachel 33
Jackson, Libby 34
Jamieson, Victoria 44
Jarvis, Robin 24

Jones, Pip...13
Kaiser, Lisbeth 34
Keating, Jess 34
Kemp, Anna 13
Kierman, Celine 24
Kilbride, Sarah 14
Knapman, Timothy 14
Kokias, Kerri 14
Krosoczka, Jarrett J. 45
Lawlor, Laurie...34
Lawrence, Mike 45
L'Engle, Madeleine 24
Lenton, Steven 14
Lester, Cas 24
Levy, Debbie 35
Lew-Vriethoff, Joanne 14
Loewen, Mark 15
Macy, Sue 35
Maggs, Sam 35
Martin, Claudia 35
McAnulty, Stacy 14
McCann, Michelle Roehm...............................35
McDonnell, Patrick 35
McMullen, Beth 24
Meltzer, Brad..36
Montclare, Brandon 46
Morgan, Michaela 30
Morgan, Sally..25
Mosca, Julia Finley 36
Murphy, Adam 36
Murphy, Lisa 36
Naifeh, Ted...46
Napoli, Donna Jo..36
Nicholls, Sally 25
Nolen, Jerdine 15
Orchard, Eric 46
Pankhurst, Kate 37
Paterson, Katherine 37
Pearson, Luke 46
Perez, Celia C. 25
Pett, Mark 15
Pielichaty, Helen 25
Polacco, Patricia 25
Reeder, Amy 46
Reynolds, Peter H. 15
Riddell, Chris.....................................15,25,26
Riddles, Libby 37

Ridley, Sarah 37
Robbins, Dean...37
Robinson, Fiona 38
Rubinstein, Gary...15
Sampson, Ana 38
Saujani, Reshma...38
Schatz, Kate 38
Shen, Ann 38
Siegel, Siena Cherson 47
Skeers, Kinda 39
Skrypuch, Marsha Forchuk 26
Smith, Matthew Clark 39
Spilsbury, Louise..29
Spinelli, Jerry 26
Spires, Ashley 16
Stevens, Robin 26
Stewart, Louise Kay 39
Storr, Catherine 26
Takeuchi, Naoko 47
Telgemeur, Raina 47
Thomas, Isabel 39
Thornton, John 21
Townsend, Jessica 26,27
Uegaki, Chieri 16
Valentine, Rachel..16
Van Dusen, Chris 16
Valdez, Patricia..39
Van Allsburg, Chris 40
Vegara, Isabella Sanchez 40,41
Wallmark, Laurie 41
Webb, Holly 27
Webster, Christy 47
Welden, Amelie 35
Wientge, Kristi 27
Williams, Marcia...41
Williamson, Joshua 47
Willis, Jeanne 16
Wilson, Jacqueline 27
Winter, Jeanette 41
Winter, Jonah 41
Wollard, Elli 27
Woodward, Kay..17
Woolvin, Bethan...17
Wynne, Diana Jones 27
Yee, Lisa...48
Yolen, Jane..48
Yousafzai, Malala 41

Index of Illustrators

Adillon, Dahlia 39

Alca, Barbara 40

Aguado, Pili 41

Anderson, Laura Ellen 27

Antelo, Marta...............................34

Arrazola, Amaia 40

Baddeley, Elizabeth 35

Barrett, Angela 20

Berger, Joe 14

Bermudez, Alyssa 12

Billon-Spagnol, Estelle 30

Binch, Caroline 12

Blackall, Sophie 19,33

Blake, Quentin 20

Boiger, Alexandra 30

Brown, Kate 43

Burrington, Stasia...............................28

Bustos, Natacha 46

Callaghan, Laura 41

Cartwright, Shannon 37

Cavallaro, Mike 48

Chamberlain, Margaret 9

Chitrakar, Moyna 42

Collins, Matt 35

Coulson, Hannah 25

De Ruiter, Jo...............................17

Diamantes, Maria 40

Doescher, Erik 47

Eliopoulos, Christopher...............................36

Ferguson, Peter 19

Gonzales, Chuck 31

Gosling, Livi 39

Green, Sarah 30

Greenwood, Francesca 22

Grey, Ada 14

Hackett, Nathan 21

Innerst, Stacy 41

Isa, Frau 40

Kerascoet 41

Knight, Eve Lloyd...............................39

Knisley, Lucy...............................37

Leng, Qin 16

Løvlie, Jenny...............................9

Lumbers, Fiona 10

Madriz, Marianne...............................39

Martin, Raquel 40

Matyjaszek, Kasia...............................11

Miguens, Marta Alvarez...............................34

Moxley, Sheila 29

Navarrete, Vicente 47

Nelson, Kadir 36

Oeming, Michael Avon 42

Ogilvie, Sara 13

Okstad, Ella 31

Penguinho, Marissa 10

Petruccioli, Rita 28

Pett, Mark 15

Pham, LeUyen 23,44

Pimienta, Jose 43

Pokoj, Ed...............................15

Polonsky, David 44

Primavera, Elise 15

Pye, Ali...............................12

Ransome, James E...............................31

Riddell, Chris...............................15,25,26

Rieley, Daniel 36

Roberts, David...............................9

Roussey, Christine 40

Russell, Craig P 44

Sala, Felicita 39

Salaberria, Leira 34

Sanfelippo, Ana 34

Scheffler, Alex...............................11

Sharratt, Nick 27

Siegel, Mark...............................47

Smith, Briony May 16

Smith, Jamie 18

Solak, Daria 40

Stahl, Miram Klein 38

Tavares, Matt 39

Tobia, Lauren 18

Tomac, Tomislav 18

Vafaian, Marjan 12

Walsh, Sarah...............................32

Warburton, Sarah 12

Watts, Marjorie-Ann 26

Weckmann, Anke 39

Weyworth, Katie 16

White, Teagan 14

Wilson, Katie...............................40

Woodall, Jenn 35

Wright Louise...............................28

Wu, Katy...............................41

Index of Titles

12 Minutes to Midnight 22
13 Hours......21
101 Awesome Women Who Changed the World 28
Ada's Idea: The Story of Ada Lovelace, the World's First Computer Programmer 38
Ada Twist, Scientist 9
All About Ella 25
Amazing Grace 12
Amazing Scientists: The Doctor with an Eye for Eyes: The Story of Patricia Bath......36
Amazing Women: 101 Lives to Inspire You 30
Amelia Rules: The Whole World's Crazy 44
Anne Frank's Diary: The Graphic Adaptation 44
Audrey the Amazing Inventor 16
Bad Girls Throughout History: 100 Remarkable Women Who Changed the World 38
Ballerina Dreams: A True Story 31
Beautiful 14
Before She Was Harriet......31
Begone the Raggedy Witches 24
Being a Princess Is Very Hard Work 14
Bera the One-Headed Troll......46
Betsey Biggalow and the Detective 18
Betsey Biggalow Is Here 18
Betsey Biggalow's Birthday Surprise......18
Beverly, Right Here 21
Brave Batgirl 47
Breakout Biographies: Emma Watson – Actress, Women's Rights Activist and Goodwill Ambassador 31
Brilliant Women: Amazing Artists and Designers......28
Brilliant Women: Heroic Leaders and Activists 28
Brilliant Women: Incredible Sporting Championships 28
Brilliant Women: Pioneers of Science and Technology 28
Bully 25
Clever Polly and the Stupid Wolf 26
Coraline 23
Coraline: The Graphic Novel......44
Corpse Talk: Ground Breaking Women 36
Courageous Princess Volume 1: Beyond the Hundred Kingdoms, The 43
Courageous Princess Volume 2: The Unremembered Lands, The 44
Courageous Princess Volume 3: The Dragon Queen, The 44
Cursed Pirate Girl, The 42
Curses! Foiled Again 48
Declaration of the Rights of Girls 30
Detective Dot......21
Diary of a Young Girl, The 32
Do Goalkeepers Wear Tiaras?, Girls F.C. 25
Dot (Creatology), The 15
Do You Speak Chocolate?......24

Edge: Sporting Heroes – Fara Williams 29
Edge: Sporting Heroes – Serena Williams 29
El Deafo......42
Ella Queen of Jazz 32
Fact Cat: History – Mary Seacole......33
Fantastically Great Women Who Changed the World 37
Fantastically Great Women Who Made History 37
Fantastically Great Women Who Worked Wonders......37
First Rule of Punk, The 25
Foiled 48
Fossil Girl, The 30
Frida Kahlo and the Bravest Girl In the World 28
Gabby and Gator 42
Galaxy of Her Own: Amazing Stories of Women in Space, A 34
George 23
Girl of Ink and Stars, The 23
Girls, The......9
Girls Can Do Anything 12
Girls, Goddesses and Giants 22
Girl Squads: 20 Female Friendships that Changed History..35
Girls Who Code: Learn To Code and Change the World 38
Girls Who Rocked the World 35
Girl Who Drank the Moon, The......18
Girl Who Never Made Mistakes, The......15
Girl Who Thought in Pictures: The Story of Dr Temple Grandin, The......36
Girl with a Mind for Math: The Story of Raye Montague, The 36
Goodnight Stories for Rebel Girls: 100 Tales of Extraordinary Women 30
Goodnight Stories for Rebel Girls 2 30
Goth Girl and the Fete Worse Than Death 26
Goth Girl and the Ghost of a Mouse 25
Goth Girl and the Sinister Symphony......26
Goth Girl and the Wuthering Fright......26
Hana Hashimoto, Sixth Violin 16
Hattie and Hudson 16
Hereville: How Mirka Got Her Sword......43
HerStory: 50 Women and Girls Who Shook the World......32
Hilda and the Black Hound 46
Hilda and the Bird Parade 46
Hilda and the Troll 46
History VIPs: Boudicca 32
History VIPs: Emmeline Pankhurst 29
History VIPs: Mary Anning......29
Howl's Moving Castle......27
I Am a Wonder Woman 29
I Am Amelia Earhart 36
I Am Harriet Tubman 36
I Am Jane Goodall 36

I Am Rosa Parks 36

I Am Sacagawea 36

I Dissent: Ruth Bader Ginsburg Makes Her Mark 35

I Got This: To Gold and Beyond 33

I'm A Girl 13

Infinite Lives of Maisie Day, The 22

Inspirational Lives: Ellie Simmonds 32

Inspirational Lives: Malala Yousafzai 35

Izzy Gizmo 13

Joan Procter, Dragon Doctor: The Woman Who
        Loved Reptiles 39

Jelly 20

Journey 9

Karma Muller's Mustache 27

Last Dragon, The 48

Legendary Ladies: 50 Goddesses to Empower and
        Inspire You 38

Legends of Zita the Spacegirl...............................45

Lighter Than Air 39

Little Bookshop and the Origami Army, The 11

Little Guides to Great Lives: Amelia Earhart............39

Little Guides to Great Lives: Frida Kahlo 39

Little Guides to Great Lives: Marie Curie 39

Little Leaders: Bold Women in Black History 32

Little Leaders: Visionary Women Around the World 33

Little People Big Dreams: Amelia Earhart...............40

Little People Big Dreams: Audrey Hepburn 40

Little People Big Dreams: Dolly Parton 40

Little People Big Dreams: Ella Fitzgerald...............40

Little People Big Dreams: Emmeline Pankhurst 34

Little People Big Dreams: Harriet Tubman 40

Little People Big Dreams: Jane Austen 40

Little People Big Dreams: Maria Montessori 40

Little People Big Dreams: Marie Curie 40

Little People Big Dreams: Maya Angelou 34

Little People Big Dreams: Rosa Parks 34

Little People Big Dreams: Simone De Beauvoir 40

Little People Big Dreams: Vivienne Westwood 40

Little Red 17

Little Robot 45

Longbow Girl 21

Longest Night of Charlie Noon, The 23

Louisiana's Way Home..21

Lucinda the Luchadora 12

Luna Loves Library Day 10

Lunch Lady and the Cyborg Substitute 45

Mae Among the Stars..28

Magic Betsey 18

Making Bombs for Hitler 26

Malala's Magic Pencil..41

Mamma Miti 36

Margaret and the Moon: How Margaret Hamilton
        Saved the First Lunar Landing 37

Matilda...20

Matilda Effect, The 24

Me… Jane..35

Molly Rogers, Pirate Girl 11

Moon Girl and the Devil Dinosaur Volume 1: BFF 46

Moon Girl Volume 2: Moon Girl and the Cosmic Cooties ...46

Moon Girl Volume 3: The Smartest There Is 46

Most Magnificent Thing, The...............................16

Mrs Smith's Spy School for Girls...........................24

Murder Most Unladylike, A 26

My Best Friend, the Suffragette...........................25

My Brigadista Year 37

My Mummy Is an Engineer 10

My Mummy Is a Plumber 10

My Mummy Is a Scientist...................................10

Mystery of the Dragon Fish 46

My Two Grannies 9

Nevermore: The Trails of Morrigan Crow...............26

Newspaper Girl and Origami Boy........................11

Night Dragon, The 13

Nothing! 13

Olivia and the Fairy Princesses 11

Once Upon a Wild Wood 15

Opal Plumstead...27

Out of My Mind 22

Parrot and the Merchant, The 12

Pashmina 43

Pirates of Pangaea 43

Polar Bear Explorer's Club, The............................18

Polly and the Pirates..46

Power of Dark, The 24

Princess and the Christmas Rescue, The 12

Princess and the Suffragette, The 27

Princess Daisy and the Dragon and the Nincompoop
        Knights 14

Princess in Black, The 23

Princess in Black and the Mysterious Playdate, The...........23

Princess in Black and the Perfect Princess Party, The 23

Princess Smartypants..10

Queen of the Falls 40

Quest...9

Rad Girls Can (Rad Women) 38

Rad Women Worldwide 38

Raising Dragons 15

Rapunzel 17

Raymie Nightingale 21

Reaching the Stars: Poems About Extraordinary
        Women and Girls......................................30

Real Friends 44

Rebel Voices: The Rise of Votes for Women.............39

Restless Girls, The 20

Return 9

Return of Zita the Spacegirl 45

Robot Girl 19

Roller Girl 45

Rosie Revere, Engineer 9
Ruby Redfort, Look into My Eyes........................20
Ruby's Wish 19
Ruth Bader Ginsburg: The Case of Ruth Bader Ginsburg
    vs Inequality 41
Sailor Moon 47
Sea, The Huntress Trilogy: Book 1, ...22
Sky, The Huntress Trilogy: Book 2 22
Storm, The Huntress Trilogy: Book 3 22
Shaking Things Up: 14 Young Women Who Changed
    the World 33
Shark Lady: The Daring Tale of How Eugenie Clark
    Dove into History 34
She Is Fierce: Brave, Bold and Beautiful Poems by Women .38
She Persisted: 13 American Women Who Changed
    the World 30
She Persisted: Around the World 31
Sisters...47
Sisters Grimm: The Fairy-Tale Detectives, The 19
Sita's Ramayana 42
Sketch Monsters: Escape of the Scribbles 47
Skyward: The Story of Female Pilots In World War Two 21
Sleeping Handsome and the Princess Engineer.........17
Smile 47
Snatchabook, The..11
Snow Sisters 14
Soupy Leaves Home 43
Stardust...16
Star Scouts..45
Star Scouts: The League of Lasers 45
Sticks and Stones 20
Stone Girl Bone Girl: The Story of Mary Anning of
    Lyme Regis 29
Storm Run: The Story of the First Woman to Win the
    Iditarod Dog Sled Race 37
Story of Ruby Bridges, The 31
Suffragettes and the Fight for the Vote 37
Superhero Mum 14

Super Women: Six Scientists Who Changed the World 34
Swashbuckle Lil: The Secret Pirate 27
Sylvia Earle: Ocean Explorer (Women in Conservation) 32
Takio 42
Tamsin and the Deep....................................43
Tender Earth 19
That Rabbit Belongs to Emily Brown 10
Thief!...19
Three Cheers for Women 41
To Dance: A Ballerina's Graphic Novel...............47
Trudy's Big Swim: How Gertrude Ederle Swam the English
    Channel and Took the World by Storm.......35
Tweenage Guide to Not Being Popular, The 44
Wangari's Trees of Peace 41
Warden's Daughter, The................................26
We Can Do Anything: 200 Incredible Women Who
    Changed the World...................................31
We Rise, We Resist, We Raise Our Voices............33
What Does a Princess Really Look Like?.............15
What Is Feminism? Why Do We Need it and Other Big
    Questions 29
When the Past Is a Present 44
Wolf in the Snow 10
Women in Science: Fifty Fearless Pioneers Who
    Changed the World...................................33
Women in Sport: Fifty Fearless Athletes Who Played
    to Win 33
Women Who Changed Our World: Grace Hopper –
    Queen of Computer Code 41
Women Who Dared: 52 Fearless Daredevils, Adventurers
    and Rebels 39
Wonder Woman at Super Hero High 48
Worst Princess, The.....................................13
Wrinkle in Time, A 24
Wundersmith: The Calling of Morrigan Crow 27
You're Amazing, Anna Hibiscus! 18
Zita the Spacegirl 45
Zog..11

The companion volume is also available from the School Library Association:

Empowerment for Girls: Riveting Reads for Secondary Schools

ISBN: 978-1-911222-23-1